BIBLE REFERENCE SHEETS

Study Guides to all 66 Books

Kevin McKinney

<u>Other Books by Kevin McKinney</u>

The Bible as History – 2nd Edition

Bible Archaeology – The Top 75 Discoveries

Bible Archaeology -and- The Easter Story

Bible Archaeology -and- The Christmas Story

Fiction (with Tom Raley)

A Dance With the Devil : The Race for St. Paul's Cloak

BIBLE QUICK REFERENCE SHEETS

By: Kevin McKinney

Hello, and thank you for your interest in these Bible Reference Sheets. These are intended to stir interest and to be a starting point for Biblical studies. For any Book of the Bible you could write entire volumes, and many have. These sheets are in no way intended to be a comprehensive guide to the Bible, only a starting point. They can be printed and used in Sunday school classes, home studies, or anywhere you or a group are beginning your study. Each sheet contains key verses from the Book, the name of the author, the date written, and various other information to help kick start interest in the Word of God.

The sheets are broken down into the Old and New Testaments as well as the Apocrypha Books which are included in the Catholic Bible but have been removed from the Protestant Bible. The sheets are laid out so they are printed on only one side of the paper, and all are on 8 ½ by 11 sheets so they can be easily printed and copied as needed. You are free to print as many copies as you need for yourself or your study group.

In some instances, modern scholars do not agree with who authored certain books or possibly the date of their writing. In almost every case I have gone with the traditional author and date. It should be remembered that in ancient times the importance of a document was considered to be its contents, not the author. For this reason, many documents did not have an author named.

I hope you find these sheets helpful and an aide to your journey into Biblical Studies. There are a great many resources available to you to continue your studies well beyond these quick reference sheets. I hope you will use these resources to study the Word of God and get the most possible from the pages of the Bible.

Kevin McKinney

Books of the Bible

Old Testament

Genesis

Exodus

Leviticus

Numbers

Deuteronomy

Joshua

Judges

Ruth

1 Samuel

2 Samuel

1 Kings

2 Kings

1 Chronicles

2 Chronicles

Ezra

Nehemiah

Esther

Job

Psalms

Proverbs

Ecclesiastes

Song of Songs

Isaiah

Jeremiah

Laminations

Ezekiel

Daniel

Hosea

Joel

Amos

Obadiah

Jonah

Micah

Nahum

Habakkuk

Zephaniah

Haggai

Zechariah

Malachi

New Testament

Matthew

Mark

Luke

John

Acts

Romans

1 Corinthians

2 Corinthians

Galatians

Ephesians

Philippians

Colossians

1 Thessalonians

2 Thessalonians

1 Timothy

2 Timothy

Titus

Philemon

Hebrews

James

1 Peter

2 Peter

1 John

2 John

3 John

Jude

Revelation

Apocrypha Books

Baruch

Wisdom

Sirach (Ecclesiasticus)

1 Maccabees

2 Maccabees

Tobit

Judith

(Additional Apocrypha Books)

Books of the Bible

Chronological Order

Old Testament

Genesis

Job

Exodus

Leviticus

Numbers

Deuteronomy

Joshua

Judges

Ruth

1 Samuel

1 Chronicles

Psalms

2 Samuel

1 Kings

2 Chronicles

Proverbs

Song of Songs

Ecclesiastes

2 Kings

Joel

Jonah

Hosea

Amos

Isaiah

Micah

Zephaniah

Jeremiah

Nahum

Habakkuk

Daniel

Ezekiel

Lamentations

Obadiah

Ezra

Haggai

Zechariah

Esther

Nehemiah

Malachi

New Testament

John

Mark

Matthew

Luke

Acts

Galatians

James

1 Thessalonians

2 Thessalonians

1 Corinthians

2 Corinthians

Romans

Ephesians

Colossians

Philippians

Philemon

1 Timothy

Titus

2 Timothy

1 Peter

Jude

2 Peter

Hebrews

2 John

3 John

1 John

Revelation

BOOKS OF THE OLD TESTAMENT

Book 1 Genesis

Author: Moses

Date: 1450 – 1400 B.C.

14% Prophecy

Creation to Patriarchs

Read Time: 3 hrs 30 Mins

The Book of Genesis was originally written in Hebrew.

Genesis is part of the Pentateuch – the first five books of the Bible

Genesis is divided into Primeval History and Ancestral History

Key Figures

Adam and Eve

Noah

Abraham

Isaac

Jacob

Joseph

Key Events

Creation

Fall from Grace

Flood

Tower of Babel

Call of Abraham

Key Verses

"In the beginning God created the heavens and the Earth." 1:1

"So, God created human beings in his own image, in the image of God he created them; male and female." 1:27

"This is the account of Noah and his family" 6:9

"The Lord had said to Abram, "Go from your country, your people and your father's household to the land I will show you." 12:1

"Some time later God tested Abraham." 22:1

"The scepter will not depart from Judah, nor the ruler's staff from between his feet, until he to whom it belongs shall come and the obedience of the nations be His." 49:10

"Then Joseph said to his brothers, "I am about to die. But God will surely come to your aid and take you up out of this land to the land he promised on oath to Abraham, Isaac and Jacob." 50:24

Key Elements of Genesis

Genesis means - Beginnings

Beginning of the Universe

Beginning of Man/Woman

Beginning of Sin

Beginning of God's Promise to His chosen people.

Main Theme

"I will establish my covenant as an everlasting covenant between me and you and your descendants after you for the generations to come, to be your God and the God of your descendants after you". 17:7

Genesis is the story of creation, but also tracks the genealogies of several key figures. When reading, notice when the author changes between families. – It begins with Adam and Eve and their descendants, then to Noah's family, Abraham's family then moves to the families of Ishmael, Isaac, Esau and final concludes with the story of Jacob's family

Book 2
Exodus

Author: Moses

Date: 1440 – 1400 B.C.

40% Prophecy

The Exodus from Egypt

Read Time: 3 Hours

The Book of Exodus was originally written in Hebrew.

Exodus is part of the Pentateuch – the first five books of the Bible

Key Figures

Moses

Aaron

Pharaoh

Zipporah

Key Events

Birth of Moses

Burning Bush

Plagues

Passover

Parting of Red Sea

Ten Commandments

Ark of Covenant

Building the Tabernacle

Key Verses

"The angel appeared to Moses out of the burning bush."3:2

"I have seen the affliction of my people... I have heard their cry... I know their suffering and I have come down to deliver them. Go, tell Pharaoh, 'Let my people go.'" 3:7

"You shall have no other gods before me... you shall not make for yourself a graven image... you shall not take the name of the Lord your God in vain... Remember the Sabbath day, to keep it holy (even your slaves are to rest)... Honor your father and your mother that your days may be long in the land the Lord your God gives to you... You shall not kill... you shall not commit adultery... you shall not steal... you shall not bear false witness... you shall not covet." 20:3

"The Lord said to Moses, 'Depart, go up... to the land which I swore to Abraham, Isaac and Jacob... I will send an angel before you and I will drive out the Canaanites... go up to a land of milk and honey.'" 33:1-3

Key Elements of Exodus

Birth and Life of Moses

God delivered His people

God brings the people out of Egypt but they quickly turn to sin.

God punished Egypt, but also punishes His own for their disobedience.

God gives mankind His laws which we must all live by.

"Moreover He said, I am the God of thy father, the God of Abraham, the God of Isaac and the God of Jacob." 3:6

Exodus shows we can have confidence that God will keep His promises and that He is the same God yesterday, today and tomorrow. Regardless of what trouble we face, God can and will deliver us, if we just believe in Him. Neither the power of Egypt nor the power of the Sea could stop God's will.

Book 3
Leviticus

Author: Moses

Date: 1440 – 1400 B.C.

59% Prophecy

Completion of the Tabernacle

Read Time: 2 hrs 2 mins

The Book of Leviticus was originally written in Hebrew.

Leviticus is part of the Pentateuch – the first five books of the Bible

Leviticus is also known as the Book of Atonement

Key Figures

Moses

Aaron

Nadab

Abihu

Eleazar

Key Events

Sacrifices & Offerings

Priesthood

Unclean Things

Day of Atonement

Laws for living a Holy Life

Key Verses

"For the life of a creature is in the blood, and I have given it to you to make atonement for yourselves on the altar; it is the blood that makes atonement for one's life." 17:11

"Do not seek revenge or bear a grudge against anyone among your people, but love your neighbor as yourself. I am the LORD" 19:18

"Do not cut your bodies for the dead or put tattoo marks on yourselves. I am the LORD" 19:28

"If a man has sexual relations with a man as one does with a woman, both of them have done what is detestable. They are to be put to death; their blood will be on their own heads" 20:13

"If in spite of this you still do not listen to me but continue to be hostile toward me, then in my anger I will be hostile toward you, and I myself will punish you for your sins seven times over" 26:27

"A tithe of everything from the land, whether grain from the soil or fruit from the trees, belongs to the LORD; it is holy to the LORD" 27:30

Key Elements of Leviticus

While God gives the Ten Commandments in Exodus, here he gives more specific instructions on how His chosen people are to live, how they will set themselves apart from others.

The Tabernacle is completed in the book of Leviticus – this is where the Ark of the Covenant was placed and where Moses would consult with God. – This was a mobile tent, since the people were nomads and moved on a regular basis.

Leviticus provided instructions on what was clean and unclean.

Leviticus contains what some would call controversial laws and/or passages regarding homosexuality, tattoos and adultery.

Book 4
Numbers

Author: Moses

Date: 1440 – 1400 B.C.

36% Prophecy

Read Time: 2 hrs 57 mins

The Book of Numbers was originally written in Hebrew.

Numbers is part of the Pentateuch – the first five books of the Bible

Numbers was a written account of the Wilderness Journey when the people of Israel were forced to travel the wilderness for forty years.

40 is considered a time of testing and is used in several places in the Bible.

Key Figures

Moses

Aaron

Joshua

Caleb

Balaam

Key Events

Numbers contains the history of the Israeli people from just after leaving Egypt until just before reaching the promised land, covering a time period of approximately 39 years.

Key Verses

"Take a census of the whole Israelite community by their clans and families, listing every man by name, one by one." 1:2

"Now on the day that the tabernacle was erected the cloud covered the tabernacle, the tent of the testimony, and in the evening it was like the appearance of fire over the tabernacle, until morning." 9:15

"Now the manna was like coriander seed, and its appearance like that of bdellium." 11:7

"The LORD said to Moses, "Is the LORD'S power limited? Now you shall see whether My word will come true for you or not." 11:23

"God is not a human, that he should lie, not a human being, that he should change his mind. Does he speak and then not act? Does he promise and not fulfill?" 23:19

"Aaron was one hundred twenty-three years old when he died on Mount Hor." 33:39

Key Elements of Numbers

God provided for the people while they were in the wilderness. He sent manna, a type of bread each morning, and sent quail for meat.

The people complained against God on at least seven occasions in the Book of Numbers, showing why they were forced to remain in the wilderness.

Numbers is a type of historical document but does not contain the legal terminology found in other books of the Pentateuch.

During the time period covered by the Book of Numbers God is training His people to be loyal and worthy of entering the Promised Land.

Balaam was a prophet hired to curse the people of Israel. He instead gave them a blessing. Verses 23-24

Total number of people in first census was 603,550

Book 5 Deuteronomy

Author: Moses

Date: 1405 – 1400 B.C.

36% Prophecy

Read Time: 2 hrs 24 mins

The Book of Deuteronomy was originally written in Hebrew.

Deuteronomy is part of the Pentateuch – the first five books of the Bible

Deuteronomy comes from a Greek term meaning 'second law'.

Deuteronomy is a farewell address to the people of Israel from Moses just before his death.

Key Figures

Moses

Key Events

First speech of Moses concerns the history of Israel.

The second speech of Moses covers both the basics of the law as well as details of the law.

The third speech of Moses covers blessings and curses in the first half and warnings and encouragements in the second half.

Key Verses

"You shall not add to the word which I am commanding you, nor take away from it, that you may keep the commandments of the LORD your God which I command you." 4:2

"He humbled you and let you be hungry, and fed you with manna which you did not know, nor did your fathers know, that He might make you understand that man does not live by bread alone, but man lives by everything that proceeds out of the mouth of the LORD." 8:3

"The LORD gave me the two tablets of stone written by the finger of God; and on them were all the words which the LORD had spoken with you at the mountain from the midst of the fire on the day of the assembly." 9:10

"Every man shall give as he is able, according to the blessing of the LORD your God which He has given you." 16:17

"Be strong and courageous, do not be afraid or tremble at them, for the LORD your God is the one who goes with you. He will not fail you or forsake you." 31:6

And Moses the servant of the LORD died there in Moab, as the LORD had said. [6] He buried him[n] in Moab, in the valley opposite Beth Peor, but to this day no one knows where his grave is. [7] Moses was a hundred and twenty years old when he died, yet his eyes were not weak nor his strength gone. 34: 5-7

Key Elements of Deuteronomy

Deuteronomy is a farewell address given by Moses to the people of Israel. It is broken down into three speeches covering History, the Law and warnings. Moses then died without entering the Promised Land. He only got to see the land promised to the people of Israel from a distance.

Moses was a key figure in many of his own writings. Moses' life was broken into three very distinct phases. The first forty years he lived in Egypt as an Egyptian. The second forty years he lived as an exile. The last forty years he spent leaded the people out of Egypt and through the wilderness.

Book 6

Joshua

Author: Joshua (and others)

Date: 1405 – 1380 B.C.

12% Prophecy

Covers the conquest of Canaan

Read Time 1 hr 42 mins

The main themes of the book of Joshua is land, and faithfulness. The two are tied together throughout the book. As long as the people are faithful to God, he will allow them to possess the Land

God keeps His promises. He promised the land to the people of Israel through Moses. Now, even though Moses has died, God remembers and keeps His promises.

Key Figures

Joshua

Key Events

The people of Israel take possession of the Promised Land

The Land is divided among the tribes of Israel.

Key Verses

"No man shall be able to stand before you all the days of your life. Just as I was with Moses, so I will be with you. I will not leave you or forsake you." 1:5

"Be strong and courageous, for you shall cause this people to inherit the land that I swore to their fathers to give them. Only be strong and very courageous, being careful to do according to all the law that Moses my servant commanded you. Do not turn from it to the right hand or to the left, that you may have good success wherever you go." 1:6-7

"Have I not commanded you? Be strong and courageous. Do not be frightened, and do not be dismayed, for the Lord your God is with you wherever you go." 1:9

"This Book of the Law shall not depart from your mouth, but you shall meditate on it day and night, so that you may be careful to do according to all that is written in it. For then you will make your way prosperous, and then you will have good success." 1:8

"And if it is evil in your eyes to serve the Lord, choose this day whom you will serve, whether the gods your fathers served in the region beyond the River, or the gods of the Amorites in whose land you dwell. But as for me and my house, we will serve the Lord." 24:15

Key Elements of Joshua

Land and Faith are synonymous in Joshua

Main Theme

God Promises a 'total' victory over enemies if we will just be faithful to Him. Nothing less than complete Faithfulness is acceptable.

"And Joseph's bones, which the Israelites had brought up from Egypt, were buried at Shechem in the tract of land that Jacob bought for a hundred pieces of silver[a] from the sons of Hamor, the father of Shechem. This became the inheritance of Joseph's descendants." 24:32

"Israel served the LORD throughout the lifetime of Joshua and of the elders who outlived him and who had experienced everything the LORD had done for Israel." 24:31

As shown in Chapter 24 Verse 31, the People of Israel experienced everything the Lord had done – because they had served the Lord throughout the lifetime of Joshua. We too can experience everything God has promised us.

Book 7 Judges

Author: Samuel

Date: 11th century B.C.

7% Prophecy

The Book of Judges covers from approx. 1350 B.C. to 1062 B.C. – 288 years

Key Figures

(12 Judges)

Othniel

Ehud

Shamgar

Deborah

Gideon

Tola

Jair

Jephthah

Ibzan

Elon

Abdon

Sampson

Key Events

The Book of Judges covers the period of time after the conquest of the Promised Land, prior to Israel having a King. The twelve Judges were charismatic leaders who lead Israel.

Key Verses

"Then the sons of Judah fought against Jerusalem and captured it and struck it with the edge of the sword and set the city on fire." 1:8

"Therefore I also said, 'I will not drive them out before you; but they will become as thorns in your sides and their gods will be a snare to you.'" 2:3

"They were for testing Israel, to find out if they would obey the commandments of the LORD, which He had commanded their fathers through Moses." 3:4

"So they put away the foreign gods from among them and served the LORD; and He could bear the misery of Israel no longer." 10:16

"So he told her all that was in his heart and said to her, "A razor has never come on my head, for I have been a Nazirite to God from my mother's womb. If I am shaved, then my strength will leave me and I will become weak and be like any other man." 16:17

"In those days Israel had no king; everyone did as they saw fit." 21:25

Key Elements of Judges

Throughout the Book of Judges, the people of Israel turn away from God, are punished, and then return to serving God. This cycle continues throughout the Book, much as we see people doing throughout recorded history.

At this period in History, Israel did not have a King, God was the ruler of Israel, but in times of need or peril, a leader would rise up and lead Israel back to God, overcome enemies, and show how faithfulness is the only path to sustained happiness and prosperity.

There are certain scholars who contend the events in the Book of Judges are not presented in chronological order. If this is true, it would not be the only occasion of this happening in the Bible. It is possible some of the events actually overlap and take place simultaneously. This in no way takes away from their historical accuracy, or their theological teaching God has given us. His word is presented to us in the order and the manner which is best and which can teach us the lesson He intends.

Book 8
Ruth

Author: Samuel

Date Written: 11th century B.C.

18% Prophecy

Takes place during the period of the Judges

Reading Time: 14 Minutes

The Book of Ruth was originally written in Hebrew

The Book of Ruth is one of the five books contained in the Megillot (scrolls). This includes Song of Songs, Ruth, Lamentations, Ecclesiastes, and Esther. These are generally grouped and read together.

Key Figures

Ruth

Boaz

Naomi

Key Events

Famine in Israel

Naomi's husband and son die, so she returns to Israel with her daughter-in-law Ruth.

Ruth converts and marries Boaz.

Ruth has a son named Obed who will be the grandfather of King David.

Key Verses

"In the days when the judges ruled, there was a famine in the land. So a man from Bethlehem in Judah, together with his wife and two sons, went to live for a while in the country of Moab." 1:1

"Do not urge me to leave you or to return from following you. For where you go I will go, and where you lodge I will lodge. Your people shall be my people, and your God my God." 1:16

"Then she fell on her face, bowing to the ground, and said to him, "Why have I found favor in your eyes, that you should take notice of me, since I am a foreigner?" 2:10

"When she rose to glean, Boaz instructed his young men, saying, "Let her glean even among the sheaves, and do not reproach her. And also pull out some from the bundles for her and leave it for her to glean, and do not rebuke her." 2:15-16

"Then Naomi her mother-in-law said to her, "My daughter, should I not seek rest for you, that it may be well with you?" 3:1

"So Boaz took Ruth, and she became his wife. And he went in to her, and the Lord gave her conception, and she bore a son. Then the women said to Naomi, "Blessed be the Lord, who has not left you this day without a redeemer, and may his name be renowned in Israel!" 4:13-14

Key Elements of Ruth

Naomi and her husband left Israel during a time of famine.

Naomi's husband and son die, leaving her a widow – she returns to Israel

Naomi is concerned for her daughter-in-law Ruth who meets Boaz

Ruth and Boaz marry and have a son

Main Theme

Be humble before God, put others needs ahead of your own and you will find favor with God.

The Book of Ruth is a very symbolic story. Ruth represents humanity, her relatives represent the Law, and Boaz represents God, and Jesus.

The story of Ruth is also a symbol of the Messiah, and how he will redeem those who turn to Him in need.

Book 9
1st Samuel

Author: Samuel

Written: 10th Century B.C.

15% Prophecy

Covers from the birth of Samuel to the death of Saul.

Read Time 2 hrs 14 mins

1st Samuel was originally written in Hebrew

1st Samuel is included in the section of "The Prophets" in the Hebrew Bible.

Key Figures

Samuel

Saul

David

Key Events

Birth of Samuel

Saul is appointed as the first king of Israel

Samuel anoints David as King of Israel

The book of Samuel is a transitional story between the end of the time of Judges and the first great prophet of Israel.

Key Verses

"She made a vow and said, "O LORD of hosts, if You will indeed look on the affliction of Your maidservant and remember me, and not forget Your maidservant, but will give Your maidservant a son, then I will give him to the LORD all the days of his life, and a razor shall never come on his head." 1:11

"When the Philistines heard the noise of the shout, they said, "What does the noise of this great shout in the camp of the Hebrews mean?" Then they understood that the ark of the LORD had come into the camp." 4:6

"Now the LORD said to Samuel, "How long will you grieve over Saul, since I have rejected him from being king over Israel? Fill your horn with oil and go; I will send you to Jesse the Bethlehemite, for I have selected a king for Myself among his sons." 16:1

"But the LORD said to Samuel, "Do not look at his appearance or at the height of his stature, because I have rejected him; for God sees not as man sees, for man looks at the outward appearance, but the LORD looks at the heart." 16:7

"Samuel took the horn of oil and anointed him in the midst of his brothers. And the Spirit of the Lord rushed upon David from that day forward. And Samuel rose up and went to Ramah" 16:13

"And so, without a sword, David defeated and killed Goliath with a sling and a stone! 51 He ran to him, stood over him, took Goliath's sword out of its sheath, and cut off his head and killed him." 17:50

"Then Saul said to his armor-bearer, "Draw your sword, and thrust me through with it, lest these uncircumcised come and thrust me through, and mistreat me." But his armor-bearer would not, for he feared greatly. Therefore Saul took his own sword and fell upon it." 31:4

Main Theme

God does not look at our outward appearance, but sees our true worth. – God will choose from among the faithful to lead His people and to do His will. Anyone not appointed by God is doomed to failure.

Book 10
2nd Samuel

Author: Samuel

Date Written: 19th Century B.C.

10% Prophecy

Covers the time of King David's Reign

Read Time: 1 hr 49 mins

2 Samuel was originally written in Hebrew

Both 1st and 2nd Samuel belong to Deuteronomistic history of Israel. Included in this group are not only 1st and 2nd Samuel, but also Joshua, Judges and 1st and 2nd Kings.

In the Hebrew Bible 1st and 2nd Samuel are one book. It was separated in the Septuagint, a Greek translation of the Bible.

Key Figures

David

Bathsheba

Absalom

Key Events

King David Victories

United Kingdom

David's Affair with Bathsheba

Key Verses

"So David sent messengers and took her, and she came to him, and he lay with her. (Now she had been purifying herself from her uncleanness.) Then she returned to her house. And the woman conceived, and she sent and told David, I am pregnant." 11:45

"And when they came to the threshing floor of Nacon, Uzzah put out his hand to the ark of God and took hold of it, for the oxen stumbled. And the anger of the LORD was kindled against Uzzah, and God struck him down there because of his error, and he died there beside the ark of God." 6:6-7

"When your days are fulfilled and you lie down with your fathers, I will raise up your offspring after you, who shall come from your body, and I will establish his kingdom. He shall build a house for my name, and I will establish the throne of his kingdom forever." 7:12-13

"Now, O Lord GOD, You are God, and Your words are truth, and You have promised this good thing to Your servant." 7:28

Key Elements of 2 Samuel

David is made King

The Kingdom of Israel is united under David

David sins with Bathsheba

Absalom rebels against his father David

David wages war to solidify and unite the kingdom.

Main Theme

Loyalty

David was a good and loyal servant of God and united all the tribes of Israel into one kingdom. He was a good military leader as well as a political leader.

David was not without his faults and the writer of 2 Samuel felt obliged to record these sins alongside the great accomplishments of David.

David committed adultery with Bathsheba, then compounded that sin by having her husband sent into battle where he would be killed.

Despite these sins, David turned back to God, repented and God welcomed him back.

Book 11
1 Kings

Author: Ezra

Date Written: 560 B.C.

23% Prophecy

Covers the times of the United and Divided Kingdom of Israel

Read Time: 2 hrs 6 mins

Both 1st and 2nd Kings belong to Deuteronomistic history of Israel. Included in this group are not only 1st and 2nd Kings, but also Joshua, Judges and 1sr and 2nd Samuel

In the Hebrew Bible 1st and 2nd Kings are one book. It was separated in the Septuagint, a Greek translation of the Bible

The manuscript of Kings was assembled over a period of time and completed during the Babylonian Exile.

Key Figures

David

Solomon

Key Events

Death of David

Divided Kingdom

Key Verses

"Then David died and was buried with his ancestors in the City of David." 2:10

"Because you have asked this, and have not asked for yourself long life or riches or the life of your enemies, but have asked for yourself understanding to discern what is right, behold, I now do according to your word. Behold, I give you a wise and discerning mind, so that none like you has been before you and none like you shall arise after you." 3:11-12

"And God gave Solomon wisdom and understanding beyond measure, and breadth of mind like the sand on the seashore, so that Solomon's wisdom surpassed the wisdom of all the people of the east and all the wisdom of Egypt."4:29-30

"And they brought up the ark of the Lord, the tent of meeting, and all the holy vessels that were in the tent; the priests and the Levites brought them up."8:4

"Behold, heaven and the highest heaven cannot contain you; how much less this house that I have built" 8:27

"O Lord, God of Israel, there is no God like you, in heaven above or on earth beneath, keeping covenant and showing steadfast love to your servants who walk before you with all their heart." 8:23

Key Elements of 1 Kings

The Death of David

Solomon is made King

Israel's Glory Days

Solomon's Death

Divided Kingdom

Main Theme

1 Kings covers from the end of David's conquest through the transition to Solomon. Under Solomon Israel experienced their "Glory Days" as a kingdom, in building, wealth and influence. After the death of Solomon the kingdom was divided and was in decline.

King Solomon, much like his father David, had a problem with his desire for women. Solomon took a great many wives, and like David this led to sin. Solomon allowed his wives to convince him to worship other gods and to even construct temples and places of worship for them. Because of this, and the fact Solomon did not turn back to God, the kingdom was divided and fell into decline.

Book 12
2 Kings

Author: Ezra

Date: 6th Century B.C.

20% Prophecy

Covers the time of the divided kingdom

Read Time: 2 hrs 6 mins

Both 1st and 2nd Kings belong to Deuteronomistic history of Israel. Included in this group are not only 1st and 2nd Kings, but also Joshua, Judges and 1st and 2nd Samuel

In the Hebrew Bible 1st and 2nd Kings are one book. It was separated in the Septuagint, a Greek translation of the Bible

Key Figures

Elisha

Elijah

Josiah

Hezekiah

Key Events

Assyria invades and captures Northern Kingdom in 722 B.C.

By 605 B.C. Babylon had conquered Assyria and also dominated the kingdom of Judah.

Key Verses

"is it because there is no God in Israel to inquire of his word?—therefore you shall not come down from the bed to which you have gone up, but you shall surely die" 1:16

"And as they still went on and talked, behold, chariots of fire and horses of fire separated the two of them. And Elijah went up by a whirlwind into heaven. And Elisha saw it and he cried, "My father, my father! The chariots of Israel and its horsemen!" And he saw him no more." 2:11-12

"Then Elisha prayed and said, "O Lord, please open his eyes that he may see." So the Lord opened the eyes of the young man, and he saw, and behold, the mountain was full of horses and chariots of fire all around Elisha." 6:17

"Now the rest of the acts of Jehoash which he did, and his might and how he fought with Amaziah king of Judah, are they not written in the Book of the Chronicles of the Kings of Israel?" 14:15

"The sons of Israel walked in all the sins of Jeroboam which he did; they did not depart from them." 17:12

Key Elements of 2 Kings

Assyria invades and conquers the Northern Kingdom

Babylon conquers Assyria, then the kingdom of Judah.

Much of the land of Israel is utterly destroyed by the Babylonian army, making much of the country uninhabitable.

With Israel defeated and the Temple destroyed, many of the people are taken away into exile in Babylon.

Main Theme

In 2 Kings God shows us just how important it is to remain loyal and faithful to Him. When His children disobey, sin, God has and will punish them. He has also shown that if they turn back to Him they will be forgiven and He will restore His blessings upon them.

2 Kings is a good example of how the people of God must at times go through times of suffering and testing. Here they lost their land, the temple and their personal freedom. God used the Babylonians to show Israel that sin has consequences, and at times they can be severe.

Book 13

1 Chronicles

Author: Ezra

Date: 5th Century B.C.

14% Prophecy

Covers the reign of King David.

Read Time:2 hrs 3 mins

All of Chronicles points to the final Davidic king – Jesus

The restoration of Israel after the Babylonian Exile

Future generations must learn from Israel's past, both good and bad.

Key Figures

David

Adam

Seth

Key Events

Reign of David

The Purpose of the Temple

People of Israel

While Chronicles retells some of the story of David from both Samuel and Kings, it does not include everything. It is much more favorable to David, omitting some of his faults.

Key Verses

"Saul died for his breach of faith. He broke faith with the Lord in that he did not keep the command of the Lord, and also consulted a medium, seeking guidance. He did not seek guidance from the Lord. Therefore the Lord put him to death and turned the kingdom over to David the son of Jesse." 10:13-14

"And the fame of David went out into all lands, and the Lord brought the fear of him upon all nations." 14:7

"So David reigned over all Israel, and he administered justice and equity to all his people." 18:14

"Then he died at a good age, full of days, riches, and honor. And Solomon his son reigned in his place." 21:7

"Yours, O LORD, is the greatness and the power and the glory and the majesty and the splendor, for everything in heaven and earth is yours. Yours, O LORD, is the kingdom; you are exalted as head over all." 29:11

"The time that he reigned over Israel was forty years. He reigned seven years in Hebron and thirty-three years in Jerusalem." 29:27

Key Elements of 1 Chronicles

Saul dies because of his lack of loyalty and David is made King

David is ruler over all of Israel for nearly 40 years

David is a strong just ruler. Unlike other writings in the Bible 1 Chronicles does not show all of David faults, such as his adultery with Bathsheba

Main Theme

The book of 1 Chronicles was written after the fall of Israel and David's descendants were not ruling the country. The author, God, wanted the people to remember the past, when David ruled Israel as a single nation in the land God had promised to them. He wanted to show they had something to look forward to – God's promises.

1 Chronicles was written during the Babylonian Exile and looks back at the reign of King David. – This is done to show the greatness of Israel under King David, and the greatness God's kingdom will have with the next ruler from the house of David – Jesus.

Book 14
2 Chronicles

Author: Ezra

Date: 6th Century B.C.

31% Prophecy

Covers the time of the Divided Kingdom

Read Time: 2 hrs 19 mins

Originally 1st and 2nd Chronicles was a single book.

2nd Chronicles was probably written after a small number of Jews returned from the exile.

2 Chronicles ends in the year 536 B.C. after 70 years of exile.

Key Figures

David

Solomon

Key Events

Solomon becomes King

Solomon Builds the Temple

Northern Tribes Revolt

Babylonian Exile

Cyrus frees the Exiles

Key Verses

"Solomon gave orders to build a temple for the Name of the LORD and a royal palace for himself." 2:1

When Solomon had finished the temple of the LORD and the royal palace, and had succeeded in carrying out all he had in mind to do in the temple of the LORD and in his own palace" 7:11

"If my people, who are called by my name, will humble themselves and pray and seek my face and turn from their wicked ways, then I will hear from heaven, and I will forgive their sin and will heal their land." 7:14

"The Lord is with you when you are with him. If you seek him, he will be found by you, but if you forsake him, he will forsake you."15:2

"For the Lord your God is gracious and compassionate. He will not turn his face from you if you return to him."30:9

"This is what Cyrus king of Persia says: 'The LORD, the God of heaven, has given me all the kingdoms of the earth and he has appointed me to build a temple for him at Jerusalem in Judah. Anyone of his people among you—may the LORD his God be with him, and let him go up.'" 36:23

Key Elements of 2 Chronicles

Solomon builds the temple in Jerusalem and God's spirit comes and resides in the Holy Place

2 Chronicles repeats the lesson that faithfulness and obedience please God and He will allow you to prosper. Unfaithfulness and wicked behavior will be punished.

Main Theme

Solomon built the Temple which was mostly destroyed when the Babylonians took the people into exile. When the people turned back to God He forgave them and allowed them to return to the land and to repair and rebuild the temple.

Judah, the southern kingdom, had 20 kings after Solomon. Eight of these kings were considered good while twelve were considered bad or wicked.

Book 15
Ezra

Author: Ezra

Date: 5th Century B.C.

23% Prophecy

Set during the Persian Empire

Read Time: 40 Minutes

The Book of Ezra picks up almost exactly where 2 Chronicles ends.

The return from Babylon is sometimes called Israel's second Exodus.

Of up to three million people who left Israel, less than 50,000 decide to return.

Key Figures

Ezra

Darius

Cyrus

Esther

Key Events

Cyrus defeats Babylon

Ezra leads a group back to Jerusalem to begin repairs/rebuilding the temple.

Ezra was a contemporary of Nehemiah

Key Verses

"This is what Cyrus king of Persia says: "The LORD, the God of heaven, has given me all the kingdoms of the earth and he has appointed me to build a temple for him at Jerusalem in Judah."" 1:2

"Then the family heads of Judah and Benjamin, and the priests and Levites – everyone whose heart God had moved – prepared to go up and build the house of the LORD in Jerusalem." 1:5

"Moreover, King Cyrus brought out the articles belonging to the temple of the LORD, which Nebuchadnezzar had carried away from Jerusalem and had placed in the temple of his god." 1:7

"For Ezra had devoted himself to the study and observance of the Law of the LORD, and to teaching its decrees and laws in Israel." 7:10

"Now I decree that any of the Israelites in my kingdom, including priests and Levites, who volunteer to go to Jerusalem with you, may go." 7:13

Key Elements of Ezra

Ezra means "Yahweh helps"

The trip back to Jerusalem covered approximately 900 miles.

The Temple was completed 21 years after work began. There was a 14 year stoppage in the building so it actually only took 7 years to build the temple.

Main Theme

God is faithful and keeps His promises. He did not forget the people of Israel while they were in Babylon, but kept His promise and allowed those who wished to return to Jerusalem.

During the time period covered by the Book of Ezra, Buddha was living in India. Confucius lived in China, and Socrates lived in Greece. (Not all at the same time of course.)

There are actually two returns from Babylon. The first lead by Zerubbabel to rebuild the temple and the second by Ezra, 81 years later, to restore the spirit of the people of Israel.

Book 16
Nehemiah

Author: Nehemiah and Ezra

Date: 445 – 430 B.C.

11% Prophecy

Covers the rebuilding of Jerusalem

Read Time: 58 Minutes

Nehemiah means "Comfort of Yahweh"

Nehemiah deals with Judah's geographic and political rebuilding.

Nehemiah ends the historical story of Israel. It will be another 400 years before Jesus is born

Nehemiah is the governor of Jerusalem for 14 years.

Key Figures

Nehemiah

Tobiah

Key Events

Temple is Rebuilt

Jerusalem is Rebuilt

People of Israel Reform

Messianic Line is Intact

Key Verses

"You see the trouble we are in, how Jerusalem lies in ruins with its gates burned. Come, let us build the wall of Jerusalem, that we may no longer suffer derision." And I told them of the hand of my God that had been upon me for good, and also of the words that the king had spoken to me. And they said, "Let us rise up and build." So they strengthened their hands for the good work." 2:17-18

"The God of heaven will make us prosper, and we his servants will arise and build, but you have no portion or right or claim in Jerusalem" 2:20

"And at the dedication of the wall of Jerusalem they sought the Levites in all their places, to bring them to Jerusalem to celebrate the dedication with gladness, with thanksgivings and with singing, with cymbals, harps, and lyres. And the sons of the singers gathered together from the district surrounding Jerusalem and from the villages of the Netophathites." 12:27-28

"What are you requesting?" So I prayed to the God of heaven. And I said to the king, "If it pleases the king, and if your servant has found favor in your sight, that you send me to Judah, to the city of my father's graves, that I may rebuild it." 2:5

Key Elements of Nehemiah

Despite many hardships, the walls of Jerusalem were rebuilt.

Nehemiah was the cupbearer to King Artaxerxes – Like Moses he gave up a life of luxury to serve the people of Israel.

Everything in Judah was restored, except for a new king.

Main Theme

Courage, selflessness, dedication to God and His people.

Once again, the faithful and loyal servant, Nehemiah, led the People back to God and to Prosperity.

While all of the Jews did not return from Babylon, the Temple was rebuilt, the city walls repaired, and the city of Jerusalem restored. It was, in effect, just as it was before it fell to Babylon with the exception that it was now without a king. The next king in the line of David would be the Messiah, would be Jesus. The city had been made ready.

Book 17 Esther

Author: Mordecai (?)

Date: 483 – 473 B.C.

1% Prophecy

Set during the Persian Empire

Read Time: 31 Mins

The Book of Esther is one of the five books contained in the Megillot (scrolls) This includes Song of Songs, Ruth, Lamentations, Ecclesiastes, and Esther. These are generally grouped and read together.

The name of God never appears in Esther

The book of Ester is addressed to the millions of Jews who voluntarily did not return from the Babylonian Exile

Key Figures

Esther

Haman

Mordecai

Key Events

Esther is made Queen

Mordecai saves the King

Jews destroy their enemies

Key Verses

"He was bringing up Hadassah, that is Esther, the daughter of his uncle, for she had neither father nor mother. The young woman had a beautiful figure and was lovely to look at, and when her father and her mother died, Mordecai took her as his own daughter." 2:7

"The king loved Esther more than all the women, and she won grace and favor in his sight more than all the virgins, so that he set the royal crown on her head and made her queen instead of Vashti." 2:17

"Yet who knows whether you have come to the kingdom for such a time as this?" 4:14

"Then King Ahasuerus said to Queen Esther and to Mordecai the Jew, "Behold, I have given Esther the house of Haman, and they have hanged him on the gallows, because he intended to lay hands on the Jews." 8:7

"The Jews had light and gladness and joy and honor. And in every province and in every city, wherever the king's command and his edict reached, there was gladness and joy among the Jews, a feast and a holiday. And many from the peoples of the country declared themselves Jews, for fear of the Jews had fallen on them." 8:16-17

Key Elements of Esther

The feast of 'Purim' was begun to recall the deliverance of the Jews from Hamah

Esther is the only Book of the Bible which looks at the Jews who remained in Persia rather than return.

Chronologically, the Book of Esther takes place in a ten-year time from between chapters 6 and 7 in the Book of Ezra

Main Theme

Be courageous and have faith in God and He will deliver you.

God does not forget His people, even those who did not return to Jerusalem.

The king kills the enemy of Esther and Mordecai and later issues a decree that gives power to the Jews and the ability to destroy their enemies. These actions were in response to and because of Esther, a very strong woman who was brave and loyal to her people.

Book 18
Job

Author: Unknown

Date: 1500 B.C.

2% Prophecy

Time of the Patriarchs

Read Time: 1 hr 46 mins

The Book of Job is thought by most to be the first book of the Bible ever written.

The story of Job takes place during the time of the Patriarchs and chronologically would fall between Genesis 11 and 12.

In Hebrew Job means "The persecuted one".

Key Figures

Job

Satan

Eihu

Ephaz

Zopher

Key Events

Job is Prosperous

Job Loses everything

Job questions his situation

Job is Restored

Key Verses

"There was a man in the land of Uz whose name was Job, and that man was blameless and upright, one who feared God and turned away from evil." 1:1

"Does Job fear God for no reason?" 1:8-9

"And the Lord said to Satan, 'Behold, all that he has is in your hand. Only against him do not stretch out your hand.' So Satan went out from the presence of the Lord." 1:12

"Then Job arose, and rent his mantle, and shaved his head, and fell down upon the ground and worshipped. And said, Naked came I out of my mother's womb, and naked shall I return thither: the Lord gave, and the Lord hath taken away: blessed be the name of the Lord." 1:20-21

"Though he slay me, yet will I trust in him: but I will maintain mine own ways before him. He also will be my salvation: for a hypocrite shall not come before him." 13: 15-16

"Where were you when I laid the foundation of the earth." 38:4

"I know that You can do all things< and that no purpose of yours can be thwarted." 42:2

"And the Lord blessed the latter days of Job more than his beginning." 42:12

Key Elements of Job

God permits Satan to test us, but only to the point allowed by God. He remains in control at all times.

Because of his faithfulness in God, Job was restored and given more than he had before. This can be seen as symbolic for the life we have been promised in Heaven if we too are faithful.

Three of Job's friends come to visit him and challenge him in very different ways.

Main Theme

Bad things happen to good people and while the root cause is Sin, the suffering may not be a punishment for the sins of the individual suffering. Through our suffering we are tested and made stronger. Our strength and faithfulness can bring glory to God, which should be our ultimate purpose in all we do.

The Book of Job is the first of five Poetical Books. These include Job, Psalms, Proverbs, Ecclesiastes, and Song of Songs.

The Book of Job also demonstrates God's power, His sovereignty over all of His creation.

Book 19
Psalms

Author: David and others

Date: 1410 B.C. – 400 B.C

10% Prophecy

Covers the time from Moses to the Babylonian Captivity.

Read Time: 4 hrs 51 mins

Psalms is the longest book of the Bible taking the average reader nearly 5 hours to finish.

Psalms is the second of five Poetical Books. These include Job, Psalms, Proverbs, Ecclesiastes, and Song of Songs.

There are 150 psalms, 73 of which were written by David. 12 by Asap, 2 by Solomon, 1 by Moses and the authors of 50 of the psalms are unknown.

Psalms was originally titled Tehillim, which means "praise songs" in Hebrew.

Key Figures

None

Key Events

All of the psalms contain some element of praise for God. The psalms cover a wide number of subjects and are of varied types.

Key Verses

"The Lord is my shepherd; I shall not want. He makes me lie down in green pastures. He leads me beside still waters. He restores my soul." 23:1-3

"The Lord is my light and my salvation— whom shall I fear? The Lord is the stronghold of my life— of whom shall I be afraid?" 27:1

"Weeping may last through the night, but joy comes with the morning." 30:5

"Be still and know that I am God." 46:10

"Create in me a pure heart, O God, and renew a steadfast spirit within me." 51:10

Whoever dwells in the shelter of the Most High will rest in the shadow of the Almighty. I will say of the Lord, "He is my refuge and my fortress, my God, in whom I trust." 91: 1-2

"When anxiety was great within me, your consolation brought me joy." 94:19

"This is the day that the Lord has made; let us rejoice and be glad in it." 118:24

Key Elements of Psalms

The Book of Psalms is actually five separate books.

Book1 – Psalms 1 – 41

Book 2 – Psalms 42 – 72

Book 3 – Psalms 73 – 89

Book 4 – Psalms 90 – 106

Book 5 – Psalms 107 - 150

Main Theme

Psalms are centered around a wide variety of different subjects. These include;

Jubilation

Judgement

War

Peace

Worship

Praise

Messianic Prophecy

There are five different types of Messianic Psalms.

Typical Messianic

Typical Prophetic

Indirect Messianic

Prophecy

Enthronement

Psalms is one of the most quoted Books of the Bible.

Book 20 Proverbs

Author: Solomon and Others

Date: 931 B.C. – Later

1% Prophecy

Time of King Solomon and King Hezekiah

Read Time: 1 hr 36 mins

Solomon wrote most of the Book of Proverbs. Solomon wrote some 3,000 proverbs, only about 800 of these are recorded in the Book of Proverbs.

In the Book of Proverbs, the word Wisdom can be translated to 'skill' and the word Instruction can be translated to 'discipline'.

Key Figures

Agur

Lemuel

Key Events

Solomon wrote most of the Proverbs no later than 931 B.C.

Hezekiah collected the Proverbs in chapters 25-29 around 230 years later.

Agur wrote chapter 30

Lemuel wrote chapter 31

Key Verses

"The fear of the Lord is the beginning of knowledge, but fools despise wisdom and instruction." 1:7

"For wisdom is more precious than rubies, and nothing you desire can compare with her." 8:11

"A generous person will prosper; whoever refreshes others will be refreshed." 11:25

"In their hearts humans plan their course, but the Lord establishes their steps."16:9

"Pride goes before destruction, a haughty spirit before a fall." 16:18

"One who has unreliable friends soon comes to ruin, but there is a friend who sticks closer than a brother." 18:24

"Many are the plans in a person's heart, but it is the Lord's purpose that prevails." 19:21

"Do not say, "I'll pay you back for this wrong!" Wait for the Lord, and he will avenge you." 20:22

"As iron sharpens iron, so one person sharpens another." 27:17

"As water reflects the face, so one's life reflects the heart." 27:19

Key Elements of Proverbs

The Book of Proverbs is intended to teach not only how to avoid an ungodly life, but also how to correct an ungodly lifestyle.

There is no biblical information on Agur or Lemuel. Some believe these are epithets of Solomon.

Main Theme

The Book of Proverbs provided detailed and clear instructions on how God's people can deal with everyday life and the challenges it presents. The Proverbs give instructions on how to relate to parents, children, neighbors, government and to God Himself.

The Book of Proverbs is a way of sharing some of King Solomon's great wisdom God gave him. In 1 Kings we hear "*Now all the earth sought the presence of Solomon to hear his wisdom which God had put in his heart.*" Now some 3,000 years later, we can share in this same wisdom.

Book 21 Ecclesiastes

Author: Solomon

Date: 935 B.C.

3% Prophecy

Covers the reign of Solomon

Read Time: 31 minutes

The Book of Ecclesiastes is one of the five books contained in the Megillot (scrolls) This includes Song of Songs, Ruth, Lamentations, Ecclesiastes, and Esther. These are generally grouped and read together.

The meaning of Ecclesiastes is 'Speaker before an Assembly'.

The key word in Ecclesiastes is 'Vanity' which the entire book seems to revolve around.

Key Figures

God

Key Events

The word vanity appears in the book 37 times.

Ecclesiastes is record of a search for the meaning of life and satisfaction here on earth

Key Verses

"To everything there is a season, A time for every purpose under heaven: A time to be born, And a time to die; A time to plant, And a time to pluck what is planted; A time to kill, And a time to heal; A time to break down, And a time to build up; A time to weep, And a time to laugh; A time to mourn, And a time to dance; A time to cast away stones, And a time to gather stones; A time to embrace, And a time to refrain from embracing; A time to gain, And a time to lose; A time to keep, And a time to throw away; A time to tear, And a time to sew; A time to keep silence, And a time to speak; A time to love, And a time to hate; A time of war, And a time of peace." 3:1-8

Remember your Creator in the days of your youth, before the days of trouble come and the years approach when you will say, "I find no pleasure in them" 12:1

"Now all has been heard; here is the conclusion of the matter: Fear God and keep his commandments, for this is the duty of every human being." 12:13

Key Elements of Ecclesiastes

To live a life with no regard for God and His ways, is a life without value.

When life is viewed from God's perspective it has new value, a special meaning and purpose.

Main Theme

Vanity is an attempt to lead a life of value and purpose outside and away from God. This type of life has no value and is a result of foolishness and the lack of wisdom and knowledge.

Solomon wrote a good deal of the Old Testament and some of the best-known Bible verses. In his younger days he wrote the Song of Solomon. In his middle years he wrote most of the proverbs. In his later years he wrote the Book of Ecclesiastes. This book seems to be a reflection of Solomon's search and the ultimate truth he learned from the wisdom God granted him.

Book 22 Song of Songs

Or

Song of Solomon

Author: Solomon

Date: 950 B.C.

0% Prophecy

Written during Solomon's reign as King

Read Time: 17 minutes

The Song of Solomon is one of the five books contained in the Megillot (scrolls) This includes Song of Songs, Ruth, Lamentations, Ecclesiastes, and Esther. These are generally grouped and read together.

According to 1 Kings 4:32 Solomon knew 1005 songs. The Song of Songs is considered the greatest of all of these.

Key Figures

Solomon

Shulamite Girl

Daughters of Jerusalem

Key Events

Wedding of Shepherdess to King Solomon

Key Verses

"I am a rose of Sharon, a lily of the valleys." 2:1

"Like an apple tree among the trees of the forest is my beloved among the young men. I delight to sit in his shade, and his fruit is sweet to my taste." 2:3

"My beloved is mine and I am his; he browses among the lilies." 2:16

"Your breasts are like two fawns, like twin fawns of a gazelle that browse among the lilies." 4:5

"Daughters of Jerusalem, I charge you – if you find my beloved, what will you tell him? Tell him I am faint with love." 5:8

"Come back, come back, O Shulammite; come back, come back, that we may gaze on you! Why would you gaze on the Shulammite as on the dance of Mahanaim?" 6:13

"Place me like a seal over your heart, like a seal on your arm; for love is as strong as death, its jealousy unyielding as the grave. It burns like blazing fire, like a mighty flam" 8:6

Key Elements of Song of Songs

At the time Solomon wrote the Song of Songs his haram was quite grand. He had 700 queens, 300 concubines, 640 queens to be chosen and 220 more concubines to be chosen for a total of 1,860.

The Song of songs references 21 species of plants 15 geographic locations, 15 species of animals and contains up to 49 words found nowhere else in the Bible.

Main Theme

Song Of Songs is a song about true love, the wedding of a King to a shepherdess and the beauty of their love and dedication to one another. Solomon uses a great many metaphors and illustrations to describe the beauty of his love for this woman.

The name Shulamite may come from the town of Shunem, which is located to the southwest of the Sea of Galilee. This area was assigned to Issachar.

Solomon is mentioned by name seven times in the Song of Songs.

Book 23
Isaiah

Author: Isaiah

Date: 8th Century B.C.

59% Prophecy

Read Time: 3 hrs 43 mins

The Book of Isaiah is the first of the five Major Prophets.

Isaiah's ministry spanned from 740 B.C. until 660 B.C.

Isaiah has been called the Paul of the Old Testament and the Messianic Prophet

Key Figures

Isaiah

Ahaz

Key Events

Isaiah speaks against 12 different countries, regions or cites.

Isaiah ministered during the reign of four kings, Uzziah, Ahaz, Jotham and Hezekiah

Isaiah predicted the rise of Babylon and their conquest of most of the known world 96 years before it was to happen.

Key Verses

"I heard the Lord's voice, saying, "Whom shall I send, and who will go for us?" Then I said, "Here I am. Send me!" 6:8

"If you do not stand firm in your faith, you will not stand at all." 7:9

"But they that wait upon the LORD shall renew their strength; they shall mount up with wings as eagles; they shall run, and not be weary; and they shall walk, and not faint." 40:31

"Surely he has borne our sickness and carried our suffering; yet we considered him plagued, struck by God, and afflicted." 53:4

"But he was pierced for our transgressions. He was crushed for our iniquities. The punishment that brought our peace was on him; and by his wounds we are healed."53:5

"For my thoughts are not your thoughts, and your ways are not my ways," says the LORD." 55:8

"Then you will call, and the LORD will answer; you will cry for help, and he will say: Here am I." 58:9

Key Elements of Isaiah

Isaiah spent most of his days in Jerusalem

Isaiah was a prophet to the kingdom of Judah, and during his ministry the northern kingdom of Israel was conquered by the Assyrians.

Main Theme

Israel, the people, and especially the southern kingdom of Judah must turn from their evil ways and wait for the Messiah which God will send to take away our sins and renew His promises to His people.

The Book of Isaiah is almost like a miniature Bible. The first 39 chapters of Isaiah, like the 39 books of the Old Testament, concern judgement upon evil men and the country which turned away from God even after He had done so much for them. The next 27 chapters, like the 27 books of the New Testament, presents a message of hope and renewal. Like the New Testament, it focuses on the Messiah and how he takes away our sins and forms a new covenant between God and those who serve Him.

Book 24 Jeremiah

Author: Jeremiah

Date: 629-585 B.C.

60% Prophecy

Was ministering up until the destruction of Jerusalem

Read Time: 3 hrs 52 mins

Jeremiah is the second of the Major Prophets.

The name Jeremiah means "Yahweh throws".

Jeremiah ministered from 627 B.C. until 580 B.C.

Jeremiah dictated his writings to his scribe/secretary, Baruch.

Key Figures

Jeremiah

Jeholachim

Hananiah

Key Events

Jeremiah was destined to be a prophet even before his birth

Jeremiah was persecuted

Jeremiah predicts the Babylonian Exile and that it will last for 70 years.

Jerusalem's downfall.

Key Verses

*"Before I formed you in the womb I knew you,
And before you were born I consecrated you;
I have appointed you a prophet to the nations." 1:5*

*"Then the LORD stretched out His hand and touched my mouth, and the LORD said to me,
"Behold, I have put My words in your mouth." 1:7*

"Then the LORD said to me, "Out of the north the evil will break forth on all the inhabitants of the land." 1:14

*"Thus says the LORD,
"Cursed is the man who trusts in mankind
And makes flesh his strength,
And whose heart turns away from the LORD." 17:5*

"For I know the plans that I have for you,' declares the LORD, 'plans for welfare and not for calamity to give you a future and a hope" 29:11

"Behold, days are coming," declares the LORD, "when I will make a new covenant with the house of Israel and with the house of Judah," 31:31

*"This is the covenant I will make with the people of Israel after that time," declares the LORD.
"I will put my law in their minds and write it on their hearts. I will be their God, and they will be my people." 31:33*

Key Elements of Jeremiah

Jeremiah was persecuted because the message he had to deliver was one of destruction and suffering.

Jeremiah was thrown into a cistern, put in stocks, publicly humiliated, put on trial for his life, and was forced to flee.

After 680 B.C. Jeremiah ministered in Jerusalem and Egypt after Judah was defeated.

Jeremiah's father was a priest.

Jeremiah was never allowed to marry.

Jeremiah was known as "the weeping prophet' because he had a heartbreaking message which was difficult for him.

Jeremiah taught not only through sermons, but also used object lessons and parables.

Book 25 Lamentations

Author: Jeremiah

Date: 586 B.C.

5% Prophecy

The fall of Jerusalem

Read Time: 20 Minutes

Lamentations is the third of the Major Prophets.

Lamentations was written immediately after the destruction of Jerusalem and the beginning of the exile.

Babylon was God's chosen instrument of punishment on His people and Jerusalem.

Key Figures

Jeremiah

Key Events

Destruction of Jerusalem

People sent into exile

Jeremiah sent to Egypt

The city of Jerusalem was burned on August 15th 588 B.C.

Jeremiah weeps for Jerusalem – some 600 years later Jesus would also weep for the city.

Key Verses

"How lonely sits the city That was full of people! She has become like a widow Who was once great among the nations! She who was a princess among the provinces Has become a forced laborer!" 1:1

"Judah has gone into exile under affliction And under harsh servitude; She dwells among the nations, But she has found no rest; All her pursuers have overtaken her In the midst of distress.: 1:3

"The LORD has done what he planned; he has fulfilled his word," 2:17

"Because of the LORD's great love we are not consumed, for his compassions never fail." 3"22

"You, O LORD, reign forever; your throne endures from generation to generation. Why do you always forget us? Why do you forsake us so long? Restore us to yourself, O LORD, that we may return; renew our days as of old unless you have utterly rejected us and are angry with us beyond measure." 5:19-22

Key Elements of Lamentations

Mourning over the destruction of Jerusalem

Confession of the sins that brought on the destruction

Future hope that God will restore the land and remember His promises.

Main Theme

The main theme of Lamentations is a sad one. The city is destroyed and the people taken away. While there is hope in the future, the Messiah will not come for another 600 years.

Lamentations can be broken down into five distinct sections.

Chapter 1 – The Destruction of Jerusalem

Chapter 2 – The Anger of God

Chapter 3 – A prayer for God's Mercy.

Chapter 4 – The siege of Jerusalem

Chapter 5 – A Prayer for the restoration of God's blessings.

Each section begins with the Hebrew letter A.

Book 26 Ezekiel

Author: Ezekiel

Date: 593 – 571 B.C.

65% Prophecy

The Babylonian Exile

Read Time: 3 hrs 39 Mins

Ezekiel is the fourth of the five Major Prophets.

Ezekiel ministered during the time of Jeremiah and continued up into the time of Daniel.

Jerusalem was actually destroyed over a period of time in three different events from 605 to 586 B.C.

Key Figures

Ezekiel

Nebuchadnezzar

Aholah

Aholibah

Key Events

Exile to Babylon

Preaching during the Captivity

Ezekiel returns to Jerusalem in a vision

Punishment for the enemies of Judah.

Key Verses

He said: "Son of man, I am sending you to the Israelites, to a rebellious nation that has rebelled against me; they and their ancestors have been in revolt against me to this very day."2:3

"He then said to me: "Son of man, go now to the house of Israel and speak my words to them."3:4

"So I will not look on them with pity or spare them, but I will bring down on their own heads what they have done."9:10

"But the children rebelled against me: They did not follow my decrees, they were not careful to keep my laws, of which I said, "Whoever obeys them will live by them," and they desecrated my Sabbaths. So I said I would pour out my wrath on them and spend my anger against them in the wilderness."20:21

"This is what the Sovereign LORD says: Once again I will yield to the plea of the house of Israel and do this for them: I will make their people as numerous as sheep,"36:37

"In a vision from God he took me to the land of Israel and set me down on a very high mountain. From there I could see toward the south what appeared to be a city." 40:2

Key Elements of Ezekiel

Ezekiel is exiled to Babylon before the final destruction of Jerusalem

Ezekiel is called to be a prophet of the Lord when he was 30 years of age.

Ezekiel is granted a vision of the new city of Jerusalem and is instructed as to its restoration and recovery.

God tells Ezekiel how the land will be divided among the tribes of Israel.

Main Theme

Ezekiel is a harsh story of the destruction of Israel and the people's exile from the land and their captivity in another land.

A portion of Ezekiel's purpose was not just to tell the story of what had happened and what was yet to come, but he was to remind the people in Babylon of their history. They had to remember the reason for their suffering, and that God would judge their enemies.

Book 27
Daniel

Author: Daniel

Date: 6th Century B.C.

45% Prophecy

Covers the time of the Babylonian captivity.

Read Time: 1 hr 6 mins

Daniel is the fifth of the five Major Prophets.

Daniel's life spans the entire 70 years of the Babylonian Exile.

Daniel was given a Babylonian name – Belteshazzar, which means, "Bel protect his life."

Key Figures

Daniel

Nabonidus

Nebuchadnezzar

Belshazzar

Key Events

Daniel deported to Babylon when he was 16

Daniel received three years of special instruction in Babylon so he can be assigned special services.

Daniel interprets dreams.

Key Verses

"Daniel answered the king and said, "No wise men, enchanters, magicians, or astrologers can show to the king the mystery that the king has asked, but there is a God in heaven who reveals mysteries, and he has made known to King Nebuchadnezzar what will be in the latter days. Your dream and the visions of your head as you lay in bed are these." 2:27-28

"Then the king gave Daniel high honors and many great gifts, and made him ruler over the whole province of Babylon and chief prefect over all the wise men of Babylon." 2:48

"My God sent his angel, and he shut the mouths of the lions. They have not hurt me, because I was found innocent in his sight. Nor have I ever done any wrong before you, Your Majesty." 6:22

He said to me, "It will take 2,300 evenings and mornings; then the sanctuary will be reconsecrated." 8:14

"Daniel, perceived in the books the number of years that, according to the word of the Lord to Jeremiah the prophet, must pass before the end of the desolations of Jerusalem, namely, seventy years" 9:2

Key Elements of Daniel

Daniel is exiled and his talents are immediately seen and he is given special instructions so he can serve the King

Daniel is found to be blameless and God protects him when those jealous of his power plot against him.

Main Theme

The primary purpose for the Book of Daniel was to offer hope and encouragement to the Jews in exile in Babylon. It was important for them not to forget their heritage and their place in history.

Daniel was approximately 82 years old when he was cast into the lion's den.

The Introduction of the Book of Daniel was written in Hebrew, then switched to Aramaic for chapters 2 through 7.

Daniel was seen to be without blame. He has been characterized by his; Faith, Prayer, Refusal to Compromise, Always Consistent, and his unquestioned Courage.

Book 28
Hosea

Author: Hosea

Date: 8th Century B.C.

56% Prophecy

Covers the reign of Jeroboam II

Read Time: 32 Minutes

Hosea is the first of the twelve Minor Prophets.

Hosea ministers in the Northern Kingdom and is written during the reign of Hezekiah.

Hosea is not mentioned anywhere else in the Bible.

Key Figures

Hosea

Gomer

Key Events

Story of the adulterous wife – symbolic of the sins of Israel.

Condemnation of the sins of Israel.

Key Verses

When the LORD began to speak through Hosea, the LORD said to him, "Go, marry a promiscuous woman and have children with her, for like an adulterous wife this land is guilty of unfaithfulness to the LORD."1:2

Gomer conceived again and gave birth to a daughter. Then the LORD said to Hosea, "Call her Lo-Ruhamah (which means "not loved"), for I will no longer show love to the house of Israel, that I should at all forgive them."1:6

Then the LORD said, "Call him Lo-Ammi (which means "not my people"), for you are not my people, and I am not your God."1:9

"My people are destroyed for a lack of knowledge." 4:6

"Come, let us return to the LORD. He has torn us to pieces but he will heal us; he has injured us but he will bind up our wounds."6:1

"Also for you, Judah, a harvest is appointed. "Whenever I would restore the fortunes of my people" 6:11

Key Elements of Hosea

Hosea has an adulterous wife who is symbolic of Israel

Israel had turned their attention to other gods which brought about the anger of God and their eventual punishment.

Main Theme

God has expectations of His people who he will bless for their faithfulness, but will punish for their transgressions.

Ephraim is the largest tribe in the Northern Kingdom so at times the kingdom is referred to as Ephraim.

Hosea's ministry spanned 40 years

Hosea was the contemporary of Isaiah and Micah who ministered and prophesied in Judah.

The primary sin leveled against the people of Israel by Hosea is the sin of Idolatry.

Hosea points out four key attributes of God, He is holy, He is Just, He is Loving and He if Gracious.

Book 29
Joel

Author: Joel

Date: 9th Century B.C.

68% Prophecy

Covers the reign of Joash

Read Time: 12 Minutes

Joel is the second of the twelve minor prophets.

Joel was one of the very early prophets of Judah

Joel was the son of Pethuel

The Book of Joel is filled with a theme of disasters, mostly in the way of natural disasters.

Key Figures

Joel

Key Events

Locusts destroy the crops

There is still hope for Mercy

Prophecy of the second coming of Jesus – the end of time.

Key Verses

"Alas, for the day! for the day of the Lord is at hand and as a destruction from the Almighty shall it come." 1:15

"Fear not, you beasts of the field, for the pastures of the wilderness are green; the tree bears its fruit; the fig tree and vine give their full yield" 2:22

"Proclaim this among the nations: Consecrate for war; stir up the mighty men. Let all the men of war draw near; let them come up. Beat your plowshares into swords, and your pruning hooks into spears; let the weak say, "I am a warrior." Hasten and come, all you surrounding nations, and gather yourselves there. Bring down your warriors, O LORD. Let the nations stir themselves up and come up to the Valley of Jehoshaphat; for there I will sit to judge all the surrounding nations. Put in the sickle, for the harvest is ripe. Go in, tread, for the winepress is full. The vats overflow, for their evil is great" 3: 9-16

"Let the nations stir themselves up and come up to the Valley of Jehoshaphat; for there I will sit to judge all the surrounding nations. Put in the sickle, for the harvest is ripe. Go in, tread, for the winepress is full. The vats overflow, for their evil is great. Multitudes, multitudes, in the valley of decision! For the day of the LORD is near in the valley of decision." 3:12-14

Key Elements of Joel

Joel was the spokesman for God during the reign of King Joash

On the day of Pentecost, Peter quotes from the Book of Joel.

Joel did not live in Jerusalem, but it is believed he lived very near the city and would have bene familiar with it and its people.

Main Theme

Joel tells the people that even though some hardships have come on the nation and people of Israel it is not to late to turn back to God and ask for His forgiveness and avoid His wrath.

Some of the disasters listed in Joel include, Plaques, Locusts, Fires, and Invading Armies.

Book 30 Amos

Author: Amos

Date: 8th Century B.C.

58% Prophecy

Reign of Jeroboam II

Read Time: 24 Minutes

Amos is the third of the twelve Minor Prophets

Amos ministered around 755 B.C.

Amos was a farmer before becoming a prophet

Amos' home town was Tekoa in Judah (Southern Kingdom)

Key Figures

Amos

Amaziah

Key Events

God Judges Israel's Neighbors

Samaria is Doomed

Israel will not listen and will not learn

Three visions on how Israel will be destroyed.

Israel cannot escape the wrath of God

Israel will return

Key Verses

"The words of Amos, who was among the sheepherders from Tekoa, which he envisioned in visions concerning Israel in the days of Uzziah king of Judah, and in the days of Jeroboam son of Joash, king of Israel, two years before the earthquake." 1:1

"So I will send fire upon Judah
And it will consume the citadels of Jerusalem." 2:5

"But they do not know how to do what is right," declares the LORD, "these who hoard up violence and devastation in their citadels." 3:10

"So two or three cities would stagger to another city to drink water,
But would not be satisfied;
Yet you have not returned to Me," declares the LORD." 4:8

"Therefore, I will make you go into exile beyond Damascus," says the LORD, whose name is the God of hosts." 5:27

"Then Amaziah, the priest of Bethel, sent word to Jeroboam king of Israel, saying, "Amos has conspired against you in the midst of the house of Israel; the land is unable to endure all his words." 7:10

Key Elements of Amos

God will judge the surrounding countries of Israel and will also judge Israel for their repeated sins. Although they could have turned back to God, the people were stubborn and continued in their wicked ways.

Main Theme

Repent and turn back to God and He will forgive you. Continue in your sin and he will punish you.

"In that day," declares the Sovereign LORD, "I will make the sun go down at noon and darken the earth in broad daylight. 8:9

--- There was a solar eclipse in Israel on June 15th 763 B.C. so the writings of Amos would have taken special meaning when the sun went dark.

The name Amos does not appear in any other Book of the Bible.

God says "I will send Fire" seven times in Amos

Book 31 Obadiah

Author: Obadiah

Date: 8th Century B.C.

Reign of Jehu

Read Time: 4 Minutes

Obadiah means "Worshipper of Yahweh"

Obadiah is the shortest book of the Old Testament

Obadiah is the only one chapter book in the Old Testament.

Obadiah is the fourth of the twelve Minor Prophets

Key Figures

Obadiah

Key Events

Edom will be Humbled

Israel will be Triumphant

Key Verses

"The vision of Obadiah. This is what the Sovereign LORD says about Edom – We have heard a message from the LORD: An envoy was sent to the nations to say, "Rise, let us go against her for battle"1:1

"See, I will make you small among the nations; you will be utterly despised."1:2

"In that day," declares the LORD, "will I not destroy the wise in Edom, people of understanding in the mountains of Esau?"1:8

"The day of the LORD is near for all nations. As you have done, it will be done to you; your deeds will return upon your own head."1:15

"But on Mount Zion will be deliverance; it will be holy, and the house of Jacob will possess its inheritance." 1:17

"The house of Jacob will be a fire and the house of Joseph a flame; the house of Esau will be stubble, and they will set it on fire and consume it. There will be no survivors from the house of Esau." The LORD has spoken."1:18

Key Elements in Obadiah

Obadiah said that the house of Edom would be 'cut off forever' and there would be no survivors from the house of Esau – When Jerusalem was destroyed in 70 A.D. by the Romans, both of these completely disappeared from the pages of history.

Main Theme

Edomites were the descendants of Esau and Edom which refused Moses' request to pass through their lands on the way to the Promised Land. These are the people who were eventually wiped from history.

There are 13 men named Obadiah in the Bible.

Some scholars believe Obadiah was the earliest of the writing prophets.

It is not known for certain, but Obadiah probably lived in the Southern Kingdom of Judah.

The Edomites left their land and became known as the Idumeans. Herod the Great was an Idumean and was named King of Judea by the Romans and ordered the death of Jewish infants.

Book 32
Jonah

Author: Jonah

Date: 8th Century B.C.

10% Prophecy

Reign of Jeroboam II

Read Time: 8 Minutes

Jonah is the fifth of the twelve Minor Prophets.

Jonah's is the only Old Testament prophet whose ministry takes place entirely in a foreign country.

Jonah was from the city Gath Hepher in lower Galilee. This means the Pharisees were wrong when in John 5:52 they made the claim that no prophet had come from Galilee.

Key Figures

God

Jonah

People of Nineveh

Key Events

Jonah flees from God

Jonah is Punished

Jonah submits to God

Jonah serves God

Key Verses

"The word of the LORD came to Jonah the son of Amittai saying" 1:1

"So they picked up Jonah, threw him into the sea, and the sea stopped its raging." 1:15

"And the LORD appointed a great fish to swallow Jonah, and Jonah was in the stomach of the fish three 17days and three nights" 1:17

"Then the LORD commanded the fish, and it vomited Jonah up onto the dry land." 2:10

"So Jonah arose and went to Nineveh according to the word of the LORD. Now Nineveh was an exceedingly great city, a three days' walk." 3:3

"When God saw their deeds, that they turned from their wicked way, then God relented concerning the calamity which He had declared He would bring upon them. And He did not do it." 3:10

"Then Jonah went out from the city and sat east of it. There he made a shelter for himself and sat under it in the shade until he could see what would happen in the city." 4:5

Key Elements of Jonah

Jonah is called by God to preach in Nineveh

Jonah refuses and goes away from Nineveh

Jonah is cast overboard and consumed by a great fish, where he stays for three days

Jonah goes to Nineveh

Nineveh repents and avoids the wrath of God.

Main Theme

You cannot escape God

You can turn away from evil and sin and God will welcome you back and relent on punishing you.

Jonah is consumed by a great fish (sometimes said to be a whale) where he stays for three days and three nights – this is referenced by Jesus in Matthew 12:39-41

The events depicted in Jonah probably took place during the reign of Ashurdan III who reigned from 773 to 755 B.C.

Jonah's story is the only Old Testament book entirely about a gentile nation.

Book 33 Micah

Author: Micah

Date: 735 – 710 B.C.

70% Prophecy

Read Time: 18 Minutes

Micah is the sixth of the twelve Minor Prophets

Micah carried out his ministry through the reigns of three kings. Jothan, Ahaz and Hezekiah.

At the time Micha was making his prophecies, Babylon was still under the Assyrians,

Micah prophesied at the same time as Hosea and Isaiah.

Key Figures

Micah

Key Elements

The Lord will Judge the sins of Israel.

God blames the leaders of Israel

God will rule everywhere

Israel will return from their captivity

God promises a ruler from the town of Bethlehem

Key Verses

"Hear, you peoples, all of you, listen, earth and all who live in it, that the Sovereign LORD may witness against you, the Lord from his holy temple.: 1:2

"He will judge between many peoples and will settle disputes for strong nations far and wide. They will beat their swords into plowshares and their spears into pruning hooks. Nation will not take up sword against nation, nor will they train for war anymore." 4:3

"All the nations may walk in the name of their gods; we will walk in the name of the LORD our God for ever and ever." 4:5

"But you, Bethlehem Ephrathah, though you are small among the clans of Judah, out of you will come for me one who will be ruler over Israel, whose origins are from of old, from ancient times."5:2

"Who is a God like you, who pardons sin and forgives the transgression of the remnant of his inheritance? You do not stay angry forever but delight to show mercy." 7:18

Key Elements of Micah

One third of the Book of Micah exposes the sins of Israel

One third of the Book of Micah tells of the punishment God will inflict upon the land.

One third of the Book of Micah tells of the hope for restoration once the punishment has been endured.

Main Theme

God is over all nations and all peoples. If we sin we should expect to be punished, but the punishment and suffering will not last forever. God is just and will never forget His promises to the people.

Unlike many prophets which minister or prophecy only about either Israel or Judah, Micah speaks to both kingdoms.

Micah makes the sins of Judah very clear. He does not simply say they sin, he gives specific sins. These included Pride, Covetousness, Oppression, Bribery, Exploitation of the weak, Cheating – merchants would use false weights in measuring in the markets and temple area.

Book 34 Nahum

Author: Nahum

Date: Between 663 and 612 B.C.

74% Prophecy

During the reign of Josiah

Read Time: 7 Minutes

Nahum's prophecy is not about Israel or Judah, but is concerned with the fall of the Assyrian Empire and their capital of Nineveh.

Nahum's prophecies come 100 years after the prophet Jonah preached to the city and they repented for their sins. – It would be another 50 years before the fall of Nineveh.

Nahum prophesied that Nineveh would fall due to a massive flood. This took place in 62 B.C.

Key Figures

God

Nahum

Key Events

God is angry with Nineveh which had repented.

Prediction Nineveh will fall

Key Verses

"The oracle of Nineveh. The book of the vision of Nahum the Elkoshite." 1:1

"The LORD is slow to anger and great in power, And the LORD will by no means leave the guilty unpunished. In whirlwind and storm is His way, And clouds are the dust beneath His feet." 1:3

"But with an overflowing flood He will make a complete end of its site, And will pursue His enemies into darkness." 1:8

"Though Nineveh was like a pool of water throughout her days, Now they are fleeing; "Stop, stop," But no one turns back" 2:8

"Horsemen charging, Swords flashing, spears gleaming, Many slain, a mass of corpses, And countless dead bodies— They stumble over the dead bodies!" 3:3

"And it will come about that all who see you Will shrink from you and say, 'Nineveh is devastated! Who will grieve for her?' Where will I seek comforters for you?" 3:7

Key Elements in Nahum

Nineveh has returned to its wicked ways and has angered God.

Nineveh will fall and the destruction will be complete.

Main Theme

No matter how strong a person or nation is on earth, they are no match for the power of God. When Nineveh angered God, her great fortifications could not save her from the wrath and destruction.

Nineveh was considered the most powerful city in the ancient world. The city walls were 100 feet high and surrounded by a moat 150 feet wide and 60 feet deep. The walls where so massive three chariots could ride side by side atop it. It was believed the city could withstand a 20 year siege.

Nahum prophesied the city would fall to a flood. In 62 B.C. the Tigris River overflowed and destroyed a section of the city walls. The Babylonians invaded through this opening and destroyed the city. Nineveh was never rebuilt.

Book 35
Habakkuk

Author: Habakkuk

Date: 607 B.C.

41% Prophecy

Reign of Josiah

Read Time: 9 Minutes

Habakkuk is the eight of the twelve Minor Prophets

God would use the empire of the Babylonians to punish both Israel and Judah, although Israel would be defeated first, the southern kingdom of Judah would survive a little longer.

Key Figures

Habakkuk

Key Events

Habakkuk complains to God about the injustices taking place and questions why God allows them to continue.

God answers Habakkuk and tells him he will punish those who are doing wrong.

Habakkuk asks God to remember to show mercy while carrying out his vengeance.

Key Verses

"How long, LORD, must I call for help, but you do not listen? Or cry out to you, "Violence!" but you do not save?" 1:2

"Therefore the law is paralyzed, and justice never prevails. The wicked hem in the righteous, so that justice is perverted."1:4

"I am raising up the Babylonians, that ruthless and impetuous people, who sweep across the whole earth to seize dwellings not their own" 1:6

"Then the LORD replied: "Write down the revelation and make it plain on tablets so that a herald may run with it."2:2

"Will not your creditors suddenly arise? Will they not wake up and make you tremble? Then you will become their prey." 2:7

"LORD, I have heard of your fame; I stand in awe of your deeds, LORD. Renew them in our day, in our time make them known; in wrath remember mercy." 3:2

"Plague went before him; pestilence followed his steps." 3:5

Key Elements in Habakkuk

Habakkuk is distressed by how wicked and sinful the people have become and questions God on how long He will allow this type of behaviors to continue unpunished.

God answer Habakkuk with a promise than the injustice has not gone unseen and will not go unpunished.

Main Theme

While God may sometimes appear to delay in dispensing justice, no sin goes unpunished and God is fully aware of what is going on and will take action in His own time. We have to remember God's ways are not our ways, and we must surrender to His infinite knowledge.

While man thinks he knows what is fair, God has His own standards of fairness which we may not understand.

God created all things, all peoples and He will decide what is fair and unfair, when justice will be dispensed and when mercy shall be given. Always remember God is in control.

Book 36 Zephaniah

Author: Zephaniah

Date: Between 640 and 612 B.C.

89% Prophecy

Prophecy that the day of the Lord is close at hand.

Read Time: 35 Minutes

Zephaniah was the great-great-grandson of King Hezekiah.

Zephaniah is the only prophet believed to be of royal descent.

Zephaniah prophesied at the same time as Jeremiah and Habakkuk

Key Figures

Zephaniah

Key Events

God is ready to bring down the nation because of His anger.

Israel's neighbors are doomed.

Jerusalem will be spared.

Zephaniah comes to the people at the last possible moment. His ministry was the last thing that could save the people, fortunately, they listened and were spared, for the time being.

Key Verses

"I will stretch out my hand against Judah and against all who live in Jerusalem. I will destroy every remnant of Baal worship in this place, every remembrance of the idolatrous priests – "1:4

"On that day," declares the LORD, "a cry will go up from the Fish Gate, wailing from the New Quarter, and a loud crash from the hills."1:10

"Seek the LORD, all you humble of the land, you who do what he commands. Seek righteousness, seek humility; perhaps you will be sheltered on the day of the LORD's anger." 2:3

"The LORD within her is righteous; he does no wrong. Morning by morning he dispenses his justice, and every new day he does not fail, yet the unrighteous know no shame." 3:5

"The LORD your God is with you, the Mighty Warrior who saves. He will take great delight in you; in his love he will no longer rebuke you, but will rejoice over you with singing."3:17

Key Elements of Zephaniah

Zephaniah comes to Judah just as the Lord is prepared to dispense justice and destroy the kingdom and Jerusalem.

Judah repents and God's anger is quitted. He will not destroy, but will instead show mercy.

Main Theme

God is slow to anger and even when our guilt is overwhelming, we can still turn back to God and receive His mercy.

The Book of Zephaniah changes dramatically from its opening to its close. In the first chapter Zephaniah speaks of Idolatry, Wrath and Judgement. The Book ends with him speaking of Blessing, Rejoicing and True Worship.

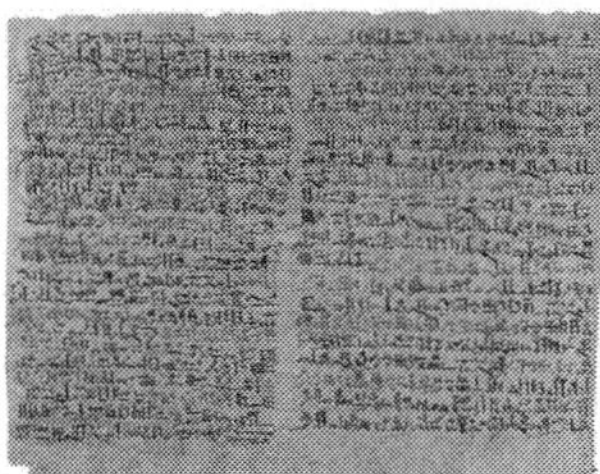

In the Book of Zephaniah, the city of Jerusalem is portrayed as treacherous and immoral.

Book 37 Haggai

Author: Haggai

Date: 520 B.C.

39% Prophecy

Rebuilding of the Temple

Read Time: 6 Minutes

Haggai is the second shortest book in the Old Testament.

Haggai had been a part of the exile and returned with the group led by Zerubbabel

Haggai was one of two prophets God used to urge the people to rebuild the temple in Jerusalem.

Darius was the king of Persia during the time of Haggai

Key Figures

Haggai

Key Events

Appeal to Rebuild the Temple

God's glory will again fill the Temple

Key Verses

"This is what the LORD Almighty says: "These people say, 'The time has not yet come to rebuild the LORD's house.'" 1:2

"But now be strong, Zerubbabel,' declares the LORD. 'Be strong, Joshua son of Jozadak, the high priest. Be strong, all you people of the land,' declares the LORD, 'and work. For I am with you,' declares the LORD Almighty." 2:4

"This is what I covenanted with you when you came out of Egypt. And my Spirit remains among you. Do not fear.'"2:5

"I will shake all nations, and what is desired by all nations will come, and I will fill this house with glory,' says the LORD Almighty." 2:7

"'The glory of this present house will be greater than the glory of the former house,' says the LORD Almighty. 'And in this place I will grant peace,' declares the LORD Almighty." 2:9

"Now give careful thought to this from this day on – consider how things were before one stone was laid on another in the LORD's temple."2:15

Key Elements of Haggai

As a part of the restoration of Israel the temple was to be rebuilt.

The temple was rebuilt beginning in 536 B.C.

Main Theme

If we are faithful to God he will restore His blessings. The Temple is a symbol of God and of His interaction with His people.

The work on the Temple began in 536 B.C. and continued for two years. Work was then stopped and did not resume for fourteen years in 520 B.C. Work continued for another four years and the temple was completed in 516 B.C.

In Haggai 2:23 Haggai places Zerubbabel in the center of the Messianic line. This will be played out in Matthew 1:12 as well as Luke 3:27 in the New Testament, when the authors present the genealogy of Jesus, the Messiah.

Book 38 Zechariah

Author: Zechariah

Date: 480-470 B.C.

69% Prophecy

Tells of God's future plans for His people

Read Time: 35 Minutes

Zechariah is the eleventh of the twelve Minor Prophets.

Zechariah was one of two prophets God used to urge the people to rebuild the Temple.

Zechariah was born in Babylon and was of the priestly line. His father was Berechiah

Key Figures

Zechariah

Key Events

God calls for the Temple to be rebuilt

Zechariah has eight visions to help instruct him on what needs to be done.

Zechariah has four messages.

There were twenty-nine people with the name Zechariah in the Bible.

Key Verses

"Therefore tell the people: This is what the LORD Almighty says: 'Return to me,' declares the LORD Almighty, 'and I will return to you,' says the LORD Almighty." 1:3

"Do not be like your ancestors, to whom the earlier prophets proclaimed: This is what the LORD Almighty says: 'Turn from your evil ways and your evil practices.' But they would not listen or pay attention to me, declares the LORD." 1:4

This is what the LORD Almighty says: "Now hear these words, 'Let your hands be strong so that the temple may be built.' This is also what the prophets said who were present when the foundation was laid for the house of the LORD Almighty."8:9

"But now I will not deal with the remnant of this people as I did in the past," declares the LORD Almighty."8:11

"The LORD will be king over the whole earth. On that day there will be one LORD, and his name the only name." 14:9

Key Elements of Zechariah

The Book of Zechariah had two primary purposes. The first was to encourage the people as they rebuilt the temple.

The second portion of Zechariah was to tell of the coming of the Messiah'

Main Theme

The people should rebuild the temple so God can reside among them. The temple however is temporary as God will bring forth a Messiah who will lead the people to true salvation.

The first eight (8) chapters of Zechariah were for encouragement while they rebuilt the temple.

The final six (6) chapters of the Book were telling of the Messiah, giving the people a hope for true salvation. It would still be nearly 500 years before the birth of Jesus and the prophecy of Zachariah would come to pass.

Book 39 Malachi

Author: Malachi

Date: 432-425 B.C.

57% Prophecy

God is Consistent

Read Time: 11 Minutes

Malachi is the final Book of the Old Testament.

Malachi is the twelfth of the twelve Minor Prophets.

Malachi was a prophet at the same time as Nehemiah

Malachi will be the last prophet to speak before John the Baptist again speaks of the Messiah, a gap of 400 years of silence.

Key Figures

Malachi

Key Events

The Lord Loves Jacob

Israel is Unfaithful to God.

Judgement Day is Near

The Lord's Day is Coming

In Malachi we have an instance of when God says he hated a person. In 1:3 God says he hated Esau.

Key Verses

You will see it with your own eyes and say, 'Great is the LORD – even beyond the borders of Israel!'1:5

"I the LORD do not change. So you, the descendants of Jacob, are not destroyed."3:6

"Bring the whole tithe into the storehouse, that there may be food in my house. Test me in this," says the LORD Almighty, "and see if I will not throw open the floodgates of heaven and pour out so much blessing that there will not be room enough to store it." 3:10

And you will again see the distinction between the righteous and the wicked, between those who serve God and those who do not." 3:18

"Surely the day is coming; it will burn like a furnace. All the arrogant and every evildoer will be stubble, and the day that is coming will set them on fire," says the LORD Almighty. "Not a root or a branch will be left to them."4:1

"See, I will send the prophet Elijah to you before that great and dreadful day of the LORD comes." 4:5

Key Elements of Malachi

The message of Malachi is directed to people who are dealing with corrupt clergy, evil practices and who have a false sense of security with God.

Malachi uses a method of questions and answers to instruct and inform the people.

Main Theme

People have become corrupt and no longer have an honest understanding of God.

The message of Malachi ends with God making a promise that things will be made right, that He will send the Messiah to redeem His people.

The last verse of the Old Testament ends with hope, but also with an ominous message as the last word in the Old Testament is 'curse'.

"His preaching will turn the hearts of fathers to their children, and the hearts of children to their fathers. Otherwise I will come and strike the land with a curse.'" 4:6

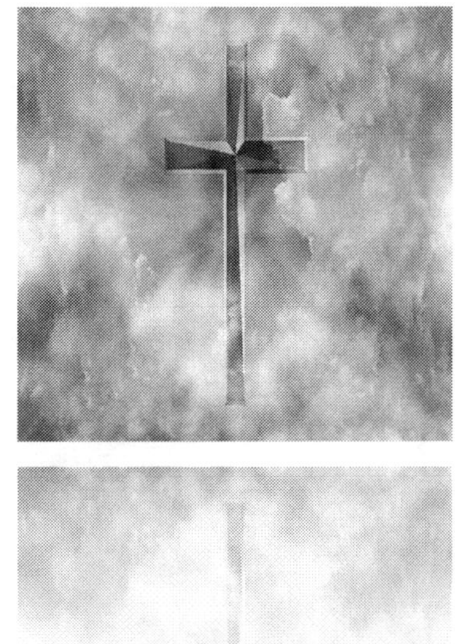

BOOKS OF THE NEW TESTAMENT

Book 40 Matthew

Author: Matthew

Date: Mid 1st Century

26% Prophecy

Message to Jews telling that Jesus is the Messiah

Read Time: 2 hrs 21 mins.

Matthew is the first book of the New Testament and the first of four biographies of the life of Jesus.

Each of the Gospels were written for a specific audience. Matthew was writing to the Jews to convince them Jesus was indeed the Messiah.

Matthew was one of the twelve apostles handpicked by Jesus and an eye witness to His ministry.

Key Figures

Jesus

Disciples

Mary (mother)

Key Events

Birth of Jesus

Ministry of Jesus

Death of Jesus

Resurrection of Jesus

Key Verses

"For where your treasure is, there your heart will be also." 6:21

"Therefore do not be anxious, saying, 'What shall we eat?' or 'What shall we drink?' or 'What shall we wear?' For the Gentiles seek after all these things, and your heavenly Father knows that you need them all. But seek first the kingdom of God and his righteousness, and all these things will be added to you." 6:31-33

"Come to me, all who labor and are heavy laden, and I will give you rest. Take my yoke upon you, and learn from me, for I am gentle and lowly in heart, and you will find rest for your souls. For my yoke is easy, and my burden is light." 11:28-30

"And whatever you ask in prayer, you will receive, if you have faith." 21: 22

"Go therefore and make disciples of all nations, baptizing them in the name of the Father and of the Son and of the Holy Spirit, teaching them to observe all that I have commanded you. And behold, I am with you always, to the end of the age." 28:19-20

Key Elements of Matthew

Jesus is the Messiah as foretold in the Old Testament.

Jesus is in the lineage of David and will be the last King of Israel.

Main Theme

Matthew's focus was on telling the Jews that Jesus was in line with David and was indeed the Messiah so it was not against their faith to follow Him.

Matthew was a tax collector when Jesus called him. This would have made him a friend of Rome and an enemy of the Jews.

The phrase "kingdom of heaven" appears 55 times in the Gospel of Matthew.

The term Gospel means 'Good News'

The ministry of Jesus takes a major turn in chapter 12 when the Pharisees tell Jesus His power comes from Satan. From that time forward Jesus's teaching takes on a different tone.

Messiah means 'the Anointed One'

It had been 400 years since the last prophet.

Book 41
Mark

Author: Mark

Date: Mid 1st century

19% Prophecy

Written for Roman readers.

Read Time: 1 hr 23 min

Mark, also known as John Mark, was a follower of Peter so it is highly possible Mark was an eye witness to much of Jesus' life and ministry.

Mark's version of the life of Jesus was intended for a Roman audience.

Mark was likely with Paul at the time of his execution in Rome, and founded an early school of Christianity in Alexandria.

Key Figures

Jesus

Disciples

John the Baptist

Key Events

Where Matthew's focus on the words/teachings of Jesus, Mark focuses more on the works of Jesus, with emphasis on His miracles and the resulting awe.

Key Verses

"I will send my messenger ahead of you, who will prepare your way. a voice of one calling in the wilderness, 'Prepare the way for the Lord, make straight paths for him." 1:2-3

"When Jesus saw their faith, he said to the paralyzed man, "Son, your sins are forgiven." 2:5

"Then he called the crowd to him along with his disciples and said: "Whoever wants to be my disciple must deny themselves and take up their cross and follow me."8:34

"For even the Son of Man did not come to be served, but to serve, and to give his life as a ransom for many."10:45

"Don't be alarmed," he said. "You are looking for Jesus the Nazarene, who was crucified. He has risen! He is not here. See the place where they laid him."16:6

"After the Lord Jesus had spoken to them, he was taken up into heaven and he sat at the right hand of God." 16:19

Key Elements of Mark

Jesus is not only the savior of the Jews, but of the gentiles, including the Romans.

Mark points out Jesus' ability to perform miracles, defying the laws of nature and science which only God can do.

Mark records the amazement of the people at Jesus' power – something only an eye witness would know.

Main Theme

Jesus came to save all, not just the Jews.

Mark writes about nineteen miracles Jesus preformed and it is done in very rapid succession.

Barnabas and Mark were cousins. Barnabas was a companion to the apostle Paul on multiple missionary trips.

Of the four Gospels, biographies, Mark's version is the shortest.

Mark spends almost no time on the genealogy of Jesus. Unlike the Jew who knew the Messiah had to come from the House of David, the Romans were not concerned with this.

Book 42
Luke

Author: Luke

Date: Mid 1st Century

22% Prophecy

The life of Jesus from a historian's view

Read Time: 2 hrs 24 mins

Luke was not one of the twelve disciples.

Luke's version of the Gospel is the longest of the four gospel accounts.

Luke is considered highly educated and a good historian. He looks at the 'facts' and reports in a very methodical way.

Key Figures

Jesus

Disciples

Key Events

Ancestry of Jesus

Birth of Jesus

Jesus' development

It is considered highly unlikely Luke was a Jew, which makes his account of the life of Jesus very unique. His faith would be based on testimony.

Key Verses

"It seemed good to me also, having followed all things closely for some time past, to write an orderly account for you, most excellent Theophilus, that you may have certainty concerning the things you have been taught." 1:3-4

"For unto you is born this day in the city of David a Savior, who is Christ the Lord." 2:11

"Why do you call me 'Lord, Lord,' and not do what I tell you?" 6:46

"For whoever would save his life will lose it, but whoever loses his life for my sake will save it." 9: 24

"And he said to them, "The harvest is plentiful, but the laborers are few. Therefore pray earnestly to the Lord of the harvest to send out laborers into his harvest." 10:2

"The one who hears you hears me, and the one who rejects you rejects me, and the one who rejects me rejects him who sent me." 10:16

"And Jesus said, "Father, forgive them, for they know not what they do." 23:34

"For no good tree bears bad fruit, nor again does a bad tree bear good fruit, for each tree is known by its own fruit" 6:43-44

Key Elements of Luke

Luke focuses a great deal on the ancestry and birth of Jesus. – He traces Jesus family tree all the way back to Adam.

Luke also focuses on the historical accuracy of the events he is recording.

Main Theme

Luke is determined to give an accurate and historical account of the events he has been told and which were spreading around the country at that time.

Luke was a physician. Some believe Luke may have been a slave. – It was not uncommon for a rich person to train an intelligent slave to be a personal doctor to their family.

It is believed Luke was never married and early church tradition says he lived to the age of 84 before being martyred.

Luke covers the first thirty years of Jesus's life with a single line of scripture.

"And Jesus increased in wisdom and statute, and in favor with God and man."

Luke wrote primarily for a Greek audience.

Book 43

John

Author: John

Date" Late 1st Century

20% Prophecy

John wrote so that you might believe and have life in Christ.

Read Time: 1 hr 51 mins

The Gospel of John is much more topical than the other three. John is not concerned with giving a chronological list of events.

Whereas each of the other Gospels were written to a specific group (Jews, Romans, Greeks) John wrote his gospel for everyone.

Key Figures

Jesus

Apostles

Key Events

Jesus calls His disciples

Crucifixion of Jesus

Jesus rises from the dead

Jesus is seen by many of His disciples and followers.

Key Verses

Jesus proclaims His deity in a series of "I am" statements.

- *I am the bread of life*
- *I am the light of the world*
- *I am the door*
- *I am the good shepherd*
- *I am the resurrection and the life*
- *I am the way, the truth, and the life*
- *I am the vine*

"For God so loved the world, that he gave his only Son, that whoever believes in him should not perish but have eternal life." 3:16

"I give them eternal life, and they will never perish, and no one will snatch them out of my hand. My Father, who has given them to me, is greater than all, and no one is able to snatch them out of the Father's hand. I and the Father are one." 10:28-29

"I do not ask for these only, but also for those who will believe in me through their word." 17:20

"That you may believe that Jesus is the Christ, the Son of God, and that believing you may have life in His name." 20:31

Key Elements of John

John stress' Jesus's divine nature and refers to 'the father' more than 100 times in his gospel.

Rather than stressing Jesus's works, John tells what the works mean.

Main Theme

Jesus is Love. He loves all of us and expects us to love one another in the same manner.

It is believed by most scholars that John was the last of the apostles to die. He is also believed to be the only one who died of natural causes.

John was nick named, "The disciple Jesus loved".

John was exiled for a time to the island of Patmos, but it is believed he then moved on and lived in Ephesus.

Church tradition tells that John cared for Mary, the mother of Jesus, after the crucifixion until her death.

John wrote four books of the New Testament, second only to Paul in the number of writings included.

Book 44 Act of the Apostles

Author: Luke

Date: 1st Century

13% Prophecy

Records the actions of the Apostles, early church.

Read Time: 2 hrs 15 mins

Acts, or Acts of the Apostles, is a continuation of the Gospel according to Luke.

Book of Acts is the Great Commission being carried out by the followers of Jesus after His resurrection.

Acts of the Apostle gives us insight on the Apostles, but places special focus on Peter, and then Paul.

Key Figures

Jesus

Peter

Paul (Saul)

Apostles

Key Events

Covers approximately the first 30 to 35 years of the church.

Key Verses

"You will receive power when the Holy Spirit has come upon you; and you will be my witnesses in Jerusalem, in all Judea and Samaria, and to the ends of the earth." 1:8

"They also said, "Men of Galilee, why do you stand looking into the sky? This Jesus, who has been taken up from you into heaven, will come in just the same way as you have watched Him go into heaven." 1:11

"Peter said to them, "Repent, and each of you be baptized in the name of Jesus Christ for the forgiveness of your sins; and you will receive the gift of the Holy Spirit." 2:38

"And there is salvation in no one else; for there is no other name under heaven that has been given among men by which we must be saved." 4:12

"Now Saul, still breathing threats and murder against the disciples of the Lord, went to the high priest," 9:1

"And he said, "Who are you, Lord?" And he said, "I am Jesus, whom you are persecuting." 9:5

"But the Lord said to him, "Go, for he is a chosen instrument of mine to carry my name before the Gentiles and kings and the children of Israel." 9:15

Key Elements of Acts

The Book of Acts begins the day after Jesus was crucified and continues until Paul's imprisonment in Rome around 62 A.D.

Covers three missionary trips by Paul and his companions. The first lasting 2 years, the second 3 years and the third 4 years.

Main Theme

Luke continues his writings on the life of Jesus which continues beyond His life and works through the lives of His disciples.

Acts of the Apostles is a natural bridge between the biographical gospels to the epistles written by the Apostles.

In Acts the question is asked very directly "What must I do to be saved?" and then the answer is given.

Act's showed that salvation was not just for the Jews, but was for everyone.

Book 45 Romans

Author: Paul

Date: 57 A.D.

21% Prophecy

Roman's may be Paul's greatest and most important letter.

Read Time: 57 Minutes

The Book of Romans was written near the end of Paul's 3rd missionary trip.

People from the city of Rome were in the crowd at Pentecost

Key Figures

Jesus

Paul

Key Events

We have all sinned

Salvation is for All people

Jesus Died for our sins

Paul's diligence in preaching

Some have said that if you can read only one book from the New Testament, it should be Romans

Key Verses

"For I am not ashamed of the gospel, for it is the power of God for salvation to everyone who believes, to the Jew first and also to the Greek." 1:16

"For all have sinned and fall short of the glory of God." 3:23

"Therefore, since we have been justified by faith, we have peace with God through our Lord Jesus Christ." 5:1

"For the wages of sin is death, but the free gift of God is eternal life in Christ Jesus our Lord." 6:23

"There is therefore now no condemnation for those who are in Christ Jesus." 8:1

"I consider that our present sufferings are not worth comparing with the glory that will be revealed in us." 8:18

"And we know that for those who love God all things work together for good, for those who are called according to his purpose." 8:28

"For I am sure that neither death nor life, nor angels nor rulers, nor things present nor things to come, nor powers, nor height nor depth, nor anything else in all creation, will be able to separate us from the love of God in Christ Jesus our Lord." 8:38-39

Key Elements of Romans

Paul preaches on four doctrines in the Book of Romans

Righteousness

Justification

Election

Sanctification

Main Theme

Jesus loves us and died for our sins. He offers salvation and hope to all who will turn to Him and believe.

Rome was the capital city of the empire and it is estimated it had a population of between three and four million people.

Christians in Rome were persecuted and put to death. The historian Tactius referred to the number of Christians being persecuted in 64 A.D. under Nero as "an immense multitude."

The Book of Romans has been called "The Gospel According to Paul."

Paul's third missionary journey went through modern day Turkey and Greece, lasted 4 years and covered more than 2,500 miles.

Paul uses the words faith and righteousness more than sixty times each in the Book of Romans.

Book 46
1 Corinthians

Author: Paul

Date: 55 A.D.

19% Prophecy

Letter to the church in Corinth which Paul had established on his 2nd missionary trip.

Read Time: 58 Minutes

Paul wrote this letter to the church at Corinth which he established during his second missionary trip.

Paul worked with the church at Corinth for 18 months during 51-52 A.D.

The official language in Corinth was Latin, but the common language was Greek.

Key Figures

Paul

Aquila

Priscilla

Key Events

Paul was writing to the church to tell/remind them of what was proper conduct for Christians.

The city of Corinth was filled with pagan temples. A temple to Aphrodite had more than 1,000 prostitutes.

Key Verses

"But, as it is written, "What no eye has seen, nor ear heard, nor the heart of man imagined, what God has prepared for those who love him." 2:9

"So neither he who plants nor he who waters is anything, but only God who gives the growth." 3:7

"So, whether you eat or drink, or whatever you do, do all to the glory of God." 10:31

"But as it is, God arranged the members in the body, each one of them, as he chose." 12:18

"If I speak in the tongues of men and of angels, but have not love, I am a noisy gong or a clanging cymbal." 13:1

"And now these three remain: faith, hope and love. But the greatest of these is love." 13:13

"When I was a child, I used to speak like a child, think like a child, reason like a child; when I became a man, I did away with childish things." 13:11

"Then he appeared to more than five hundred brothers at one time, most of whom are still alive, though some have fallen asleep. Then he appeared to James, then to all the apostles. Last of all, as to one untimely born, he appeared also to me." 15: 6-8

Key Elements

Let how you live be an example to others.

Remember what you have learned and do not fall back into the old ways/sins.

Become a mature adult Christian.

Main Theme

Jesus loves you, and you should love one another.

There is a strong possibility there is a missing letter from Paul to the church at Corinth which was written prior to 1 Corinthians. We see in chapter 5 verse 9 that Paul makes a reference to the potential letter.

"I wrote to you in my letter not to associate with sexually immoral people," 5:9

It is possible this is a known letter of Paul which is to a different church but was to be distributed to and read at the church at Corinth.

Paul stress's that the freedom of Christians was bought by the blood of Christ and we should always remember and respect this fact.

Book 47

2 Corinthians

Author: Paul

Date: 56 A.D.

5% Prophecy

Paul defends his authority

Read Time: 38 Minutes

After Paul's first letter to the church in Corinth a number of false teachers began making trouble. In order to resolve the issues and calm the church Paul wrote this second letter to the church in Corinth.

Paul would eventually visit Corinth a third time in hopes of providing strength to the church.

Key Figures

Paul

Titus

Key Events

Never Give up Hope

Lesson on faithful giving

Paul's authority as an Apostle

Paul wants to visit Corinth again.

Paul's Labors and Sufferings

Key Verses

"For we know that if the earthly tent we live in is destroyed, we have a building from God, an eternal house in heaven, not built by human hands." 5:1

"Therefore, if anyone is in Christ, the new creation has come: The old has gone, the new is here!" 5:21

"Do not be yoked together with unbelievers. For what do righteousness and wickedness have in common? Or what fellowship can light have with darkness?" 6:14

"Remember this: Whoever sows sparingly will also reap sparingly, and whoever sows generously will also reap generously." 9:6

"Each of you should give what you have decided in your heart to give, not reluctantly or under compulsion, for God loves a cheerful giver." 9:7

"And I will keep on doing what I am doing in order to cut the ground from under those who want an opportunity to be considered equal with us in the things they boast about." 11:12

Key Elements of 2 Corinthians

Paul is struggling against false teachers and must set the church back on the right track by assuring them of his authority, the accuracy of his message, and the power they have through their faith.

Paul gives a lengthy testimony about giving in verses 8-9, perhaps the longest discussion of giving found in the New Testament.

Main Theme

The message Paul is delivering is accurate, true, and the only way to salvation.

The second letter to the Corinthians was delivered to the church by Titus and another brother.

The city of Corinth was destroyed in 146 B.C. by the Romans. It was rebuilt 100 years later by Julius Caesar as the capital of Achaia.

More than sixty percent of the population of Corinth were slaves.

Corinth was famous for its shrines, prostitutes and debauchery.

Book 48 Galatians

Author: Paul

Date: 49 A.D.

11% Prophecy

Written during Paul's first missionary Journey.

Read Time: 20 Minutes

Paul dictated most of his letters to scribes. It is believed Paul wrote this letter in his own hand.

Galatians has been called the Christians Declaration of Independence as well as the Magna Carta of Christianity.

Key Figures

Paul

Key Events

Paul's Call to Ministry

In Jerusalem

Paul confronts Peter

Purpose of the Law

Privilege of Christian Liberty

The Practice of the Law

Sowing and Reaping

Closing Remarks

Key Verses

"But even if we or an angel from heaven should preach a gospel other than the one we preached to you, let that person be under God's curse!" 1:8

"Know that a person is not justified by observing the law, but by faith in Jesus Christ. So we, too, have put our faith in Christ Jesus that we may be justified by faith in Christ and not by observing the law, because by observing the law no one will be justified." 2:16

"So the law was put in charge of us until Christ came that we might be justified by faith." 3:24

"There is neither Jew nor Gentile, neither slave nor free, neither male nor female, for you are all one in Christ Jesus" 3:28

"For in Christ Jesus neither circumcision nor uncircumcision has any value. The only thing that counts is faith expressing itself through love." 5:6

"Let us not become weary in doing good, for at the proper time we will reap a harvest if we do not give up." 6:9

Key Elements of Galatians

Paul preaches that we have freedom in Christ. He makes it very clear that with the coming of Christ, His death and resurrection, all who follow Him are free from sin, free from the doctrine of men, and free from the Laws of Moses.

The law of Moses was given to man by God as a temporary means to show praise and loyalty to God until the Messiah, Jesus, came.

Main Theme

Jesus did not come for any one group of people or a single nation. Jesus came to save everyone, and His salvation is open to everyone, Jew and Gentile equally.

Galatians was written as a response to teachers who were proclaiming Jesus as the Messiah, but who were also telling the gentiles they would have to follow the Jewish laws and customs in order to receive a share in the salvation offered by Jesus. Paul made it as clear as he could that this was a false teaching.

In Galatians, Paul refers to 'the law' a total of 31 times. This was key to his message that the law had been replaced by the saving grace of Jesus.

Book 49 Ephesians

Author: Paul

Date: 61 A.D.

5% Prophecy

Written during Paul's Imprisonment

Read Time: 10 Minutes

Ephesians is one of four letters Paul wrote while he was in prison in Rome. These are known as the 'prison Epistles' and included Ephesians, Philippians, Colossians, and Philemon.

During his third missionary trip Paul spent three years in Ephesus

Key Figures

Paul

Key Events

God's purpose in Christ

Paul's Prayer for the Ephesians

A new way of thinking

Husbands and Wives

Children and Parents

Servants and Masters

The Christian's Armor

Walk in Love

Key Verses

"Even as he chose us in him before the foundation of the world, that we should be holy and blameless before him. In love he predestined us for adoption as sons through Jesus Christ, according to the purpose of his will." 1: 4-5

"In him we have redemption through his blood, the forgiveness of our trespasses, according to the riches of his grace, which he lavished upon us, in all wisdom and insight." 1: 7-8

"Making known to us the mystery of his will, according to his purpose, which he set forth in Christ." 1:9

"God, being rich in mercy, because of the great love with which he loved us, even when we were dead in our trespasses, made us alive together with Christ—by grace you have been saved." 2: 4-5

"For by grace you have been saved through faith. And this is not your own doing; it is the gift of God, not a result of works, so that no one may boast." 2: 8-9

"Therefore a man shall leave his father and mother and hold fast to his wife, and the two shall become one flesh." This mystery is profound, and I am saying that it refers to Christ and the church." 5: 31-32

Key Elements in Ephesians

Paul shows that God sent Jesus to us not after we had repented, not after we had thrown off sin, but while we were still sinners, while we were undeserving, God sent Jesus to save us.

Because we were sinners, we cannot boast about our salvation as it was a free gift from God which none of us deserved.

Main Theme

Paul makes seven very important points in this epistle. He points out the seven 'Ones". Paul instructs us that there is One body, one spirit, one hope, one lord, one faith, one baptism and one God.

Paul tells us to put on our Full Armor of God for we are in a war, a daily struggle.

"For our struggle is not against flesh and blood, but against the rulers, against the powers, against the world forces of this darkness, against the spiritual forces of wickedness in the heavenly places." 6:12

Paul tells us our armor must include many things, but above all else we must take up the Shield of Faith, for there is no substitution for faith. It is the one thing we can and are to give to God.

Book 50 Philippians

Author: Paul

Date: 62 A.D.

10% Prophecy

For me to live in Christ, and to die is gain.

Read Time: 14 Minutes

Philippians is one of four letters Paul wrote while he was in prison in Rome. These are known as the 'prison Epistles' and included Ephesians, Philippians, Colossians, and Philemon.

Paul travelled to Philippi in 51 A.D. with Luke, Timothy and Silas

This letter was more to say thank you to the church at Philippi for their generous support rather than to teach doctrine.

Key Figures

Paul

Key Events

Be Like Christ

Count all gains as lose

The High Calling of God

Rejoice in the Lord

Contentment

Key Verses

"Who, though he was in the form of God, did not count equality with God a thing to be grasped, but emptied himself, by taking the form of a servant, being born in the likeness of men." 2: 6-7

"And being found in human form, he humbled himself by becoming obedient to the point of death, even death on a cross." 2:8

"That I may know him and the power of his resurrection, and may share his sufferings, becoming like him in his death." 3:10

"Brothers, I do not consider that I have made it my own. But one thing I do: forgetting what lies behind and straining forward to what lies ahead, I press on toward the goal for the prize of the upward call of God in Christ Jesus." 3: 13-14

"But our citizenship is in heaven, and from it we await a Savior, the Lord Jesus Christ, who will transform our lowly body to be like his glorious body, by the power that enables him even to subject all things to himself." 3: 20-21

"Do not be anxious about anything, but in everything by prayer and supplication with thanksgiving let your requests be made known to God." 4:7

Key Elements of Philippians

The Philippi church was the first established by Paul in Europe.

Paul visited Philippi on his first and third missionary journey.

Each chapter in Philippians has a definite theme. – Chapter one – Christ is Life, Chapter two – Christ is our example, Chapter three – Christ is our hope, Chapter four – Christ is our strength.

Main Theme

"I can do all things through Christ who strengthens me." 4:13

The Letter to the Philippians was delivered to Philippi from Rome by Epaphroditus.

The city of Philippi was named for Philippi Macedon who was the father of Alexander the Great.

The Romans captured the city of Philippi in 168 B.C. and turned it into a Roman colony and established a military outpost there as well.

Book 51 Colossians

Author: Paul

Date: 61 A.D.

9% Prophecy

Focus on the Head of the church, which is Jesus.

Read Time: 13 Minutes

Colossians is one of four letters Paul wrote while he was in prison in Rome. These are known as the 'prison Epistles' and included Ephesians, Philippians, Colossians, and Philemon.

The church at Colosse was established by Epaphras and at the time of writing this letter Paul had not yet visited this church or the city.

The church of Colosse was in the region of the seven churches of Asia.

Key Figures

Jesus

Paul

Key Events

The Letter to the Colossians focuses on Christ Jesus, the Head of the church.

Paul wanted this letter read to the surrounding churches so it was a regional letter.

Key Verses

"He is the image of the invisible God, the firstborn of all creation. For by him all things were created, in heaven and on earth, visible and invisible, whether thrones or dominions or rulers or authorities—all things were created through him and for him." 1:15-16

"Once you were alienated from God and were enemies in your minds because of[a] your evil behavior. 22 But now he has reconciled you by Christ's physical body through death to present you holy in his sight, without blemish and free from accusation" 1:21-22

"See to it that no one takes you captive through hollow and deceptive philosophy, which depends on human tradition and the elemental spiritual forces[a] of this world rather than on Christ." 2:8

"Therefore do not let anyone judge you by what you eat or drink, or with regard to a religious festival, a New Moon celebration or a Sabbath day. 17 These are a shadow of the things that were to come; the reality, however, is found in Christ." 2:16-17

"Here there is no Gentile or Jew, circumcised or uncircumcised, barbarian, Scythian, slave or free, but Christ is all, and is in all." 3:11

Key Elements of Colossians

The life, death and resurrection of Jesus has freed us from human rules. We are bound only by the rules of God.

Jesus is the head of the church, it was His sacrifice that bought our freedom through the plan and will of God.

Main Theme

Focus on Jesus, not philosophy, nationality, race, or earthly deeds. Focus on Jesus, who is the ultimate prize.

Paul wrote the letter to the Colossians in Rome. It was delivered to Colosse by Tychicus and Onesimus who was a converted slave.

Paul uses different language and tones for each of his letters. In the letter to the Colossians Paul uses 55 Greek words that do not appear in any of his other letters.

Colosse was a very populated area which was famous throughout the known world for its glossy black wool.

Colosse was about 100 miles from Ephesus

Book 52 1 Thessalonians

Author: Paul

Date: 51 A.D.

18% Prophecy

Comfort one another until the return of Jesus

Read Time: 11 Minutes

1 Thessalonians was the first letter Paul wrote. – He would eventually write a total of 13 letters which appear in the New Testament. It is believed by some there may be at least two letters which were lost and did not get included in the Bible text.

Paul was forced to leave Thessalonica but he continued to be very interested in the church.

Key Figures

Jesus

Paul

Key Events

Power of the Gospel

The Rapture

Stand fast in belief

Sanctification

Key Verses

"And we also thank God continually because, when you received the word of God, which you heard from us, you accepted it not as a human word, but as it actually is, the word of God, which is indeed at work in you who believe." 2:13

"Brothers and sisters, we do not want you to be uninformed about those who sleep in death, so that you do not grieve like the rest, who have no hope." 4:13

"Then we who are alive, who are left, will be caught up together with them in the clouds to meet the Lord in the air, and so we will always be with the Lord. Therefore encourage one another with these words." 4:17

"He died for us so that, whether we are awake or asleep, we may live together with him." 5:10

Therefore encourage one another and build each other up, just as in fact you are doing."5:11

"Do not put out the Spirit's fire." 5:19

"But test them all; hold on to what is good" 5:21

Key Elements of 1 Thessalonians

This letter is somewhat different from Paul's other letters. He is complementing the believers for doing well after his departure.

Paul discusses the brothers and sisters who have gone before us and who now sleep in Christ. He gives reassurance they are not lost and hope remains.

Main Theme

"Pray continually" 5:17

Thessalonica was located about 100 miles from Philippi on the great northern highway from Rome to the east.

Paul's dual purpose in the letter was to commend the church for holding to the teaching, and to console them for the lost loved ones.

Paul discusses the return of Jesus in 1 Thessalonians. It is a common subject as it appears in 23 of the 27 books of the New Testament.

Paul was kept up to date on the progress and condition of the church as Thessalonica by Timothy.

Book 53

2 Thessalonians

Author: Paul

Date: 51 A.D.

40% Prophecy

Written to address false teaches that had crept into the church

---

Read Time: 7 Minutes

---

2 Thessalonians was the second letter written to the church in Thessalonica and was the second letter Paul wrote overall. He would author 13 letters that appear in the New Testament.

This is the shortest letter Paul wrote to any church or congregation.

Paul established the church at Thessalonica during his second missionary journey.

Key Figures

Jesus

Paul

Key Events

Mystery of Iniquity

Stand Firm

Key verses

"All this is evidence that God's judgment is right, and as a result you will be counted worthy of the kingdom of God, for which you are suffering." 1:5

"And give relief to you who are troubled, and to us as well. This will happen when the Lord Jesus is revealed from heaven in blazing fire with his powerful angels." 1:7

"The coming of the lawless one will be in accordance with how Satan works. He will use all sorts of displays of power through signs and wonders that serve the lie" 2:9

"And so that all will be condemned who have not believed the truth but have delighted in wickedness." 2:12

"In the name of the Lord Jesus Christ, we command you, brothers and sisters, to keep away from every believer who is idle and disruptive and does not live according to the teaching you received from us." 3:6

"Such people we command and urge in the Lord Jesus Christ to settle down and earn the bread they eat." 3:12

Key Elements of 2 Thessalonians

Jesus will return as He promised, but it will be in His time and when it is the proper time.

Christians should not be of this world and should not try to fit into this world. We are a people set apart by the saving grace of Jesus.

We should not associate with people who do evil or teach something other than the gospel of Jesus. These people are a danger to ensnare us and lead us away from the truth.

Main Theme

"But as for you, brethren, do not grow weary in doing good." 3:13

Thessalonica was the Capital of the Roman province of Macedonia.

Thessalonica was a very prominent sea port and traded throughout the region. This contributed to its size and a diverse population.

Its diverse population could have been a cause of such a variety of beliefs which Paul warned the church about.

Book 54
1 Timothy

Author: Paul

Date: 64 A.D.

4% Prophecy

Written after Paul's first imprisonment.

Read Time: 15 Minutes

The last three letters or Epistles written by Paul are known as the "Pastoral Epistles." This includes 1 Timothy, Titus and 2 Timothy.

Timothy was converted during Paul's first missionary journey. He was a native of Lystra where Paul was stoned.

On Paul's second missionary journey he visited Lystra again and took Timothy with him to help with the work.

Key Figures

Paul

Timothy

Key Events

False Doctrine

Qualifications for Bishop

Qualifications for Deacon

Healthy Teaching

Key Verses

"The saying is trustworthy and deserving of full acceptance, that Christ Jesus came into the world to save sinners, of whom I am the foremost."1:15

"First of all, then, I urge that supplications, prayers, intercessions, and thanksgivings be made for all people, for kings and all who are in high positions, that we may lead a peaceful and quiet life, godly and dignified in every way." 2:1-2

"For there is one God, and there is one mediator between God and men, the man Christ Jesus, who gave himself as a ransom for all, which is the testimony given at the proper time." 2: 5-6

"Therefore an overseer must be above reproach, the husband of one wife, sober-minded, self-controlled, respectable, hospitable, able to teach, not a drunkard, not violent but gentle, not quarrelsome, not a lover of money." 3:2-3

"Now the Spirit expressly says that in later times some will depart from the faith by devoting themselves to deceitful spirits and teachings of demons, through the insincerity of liars whose consciences are seared." 4:1-2

"Let no one despise you for your youth, but set the believers an example in speech, in conduct, in love, in faith, in purity. Until I come, devote yourself to the public reading of Scripture, to exhortation, to teaching." 4: 12-13

Keu Elements of 1 Timothy

Church organizations, including elders, deacons and bishops.

Timothy was instructed to teach the truth above all else and to correct others when they were in error, despite his youth.

Main Theme

Timothy was to oversee the organization of the church.

The law of Moses ended with the coming of the Messiah, Jesus, but Timothy was still circumcised because of the work they would be doing and to help prevent controversy. They wanted the focus to be on the Gospel, not about Timothy.

Timothy's father was a Greek, his mother was Eunice.

According to Hebrews, Timothy was imprisoned at some point, presumably due to his faith in Jesus.

"Fight the good fight of the faith. Take hold of the eternal life to which you were called when you made your good confession in the presence of many witnesses." 6:12

Book 55
2 Timothy

Author: Paul

Date: 67 A.D.

20% Prophecy

Faithful Ministry

Read Time: 11 Minutes

2 Timothy was the last letter Paul would write. It was written from his prison cell in Rome

The last three letters or Epistles written by Paul are known as the "Pastoral Epistles." This includes 1 Timothy, Titus and 2 Timothy.

This was Paul's second trial in Rome and he would be put to death shortly after writing this letter.

Key Figures

Paul

Timothy

Luke

Key Events

The Christian Warfare

The Last Times

Scriptures are Inspired

Paul's closing words

Key Verses

"What you heard from me, keep as the pattern of sound teaching, with faith and love in Christ Jesus." 1:13

"For which I am suffering even to the point of being chained like a criminal. But God's word is not chained." 2:9

"Here is a trustworthy saying: If we died with him, we will also live with him" 2:11

"All Scripture is God-breathed and is useful for teaching, rebuking, correcting and training in righteousness"3:16

"But mark this: There will be terrible times in the last days." 3:1

"For the time will come when people will not put up with sound doctrine. Instead, to suit their own desires, they will gather around them a great number of teachers to say what their itching ears want to hear." 4:3

"I have fought the good fight, I have finished the race, I have kept the faith." 4:7

"When you come, bring the cloak that I left with Carpus at Troas, and my scrolls, especially the parchments." 4:13

Key Elements of 2 Timothy

Paul is in prison and awaiting his execution. He knows his death is not far off and is trying to complete what tasks he can.

Despite his own circumstances, Paul still encourages the others to continue the fight and be encouraged that Jesus will never forsake them.

Main Theme

Paul's time on this earth is all but done, he must prepare the others who will carry on the fight once he is gone.

Paul requests his books and parchments to be brought to him. What books and writings were included in this collection are unknown.

Paul calls Timothy a Good Soldier, and obviously holds him in very high regard.

It is believed Timothy and perhaps Mark and Luke had reached Rome and were with Paul when he was executed, but this cannot be confirmed.

Book 56 Titus

Author: Paul

Date: 65 A.D.

2% Prophecy

During the time of the early church in Crete

Read Time: 6 Minutes

Paul sent Titus to Corinth on three different occasions.

It is believed Titus was a covert of Paul

Titus is mentioned 13 times in the letters of Paul but is not mentioned at all by Luke in the Book of Acts.

Key Figures

Paul

Titus

Key Events

Qualifications of an elder

Teach sound doctrine

Rapture of the church

Exhortation to Good Works

Key Verses

"In the hope of eternal life, which God, who does not lie, promised before the beginning of time" 1:2

"The reason I left you in Crete was that you might put in order what was left unfinished and appoint elders in every town, as I directed you." 1:5

"And will pay no attention to Jewish myths or to the merely human commands of those who reject the truth." 1:14

"Similarly, encourage the young men to be self-controlled." 2:6

"Remind the people to be subject to rulers and authorities, to be obedient, to be ready to do whatever is good" 3:1

"He saved us, not because of righteous things we had done, but because of his mercy. He saved us through the washing of rebirth and renewal by the Holy Spirit" 3:5

"But avoid foolish controversies and genealogies and arguments and quarrels about the law, because these are unprofitable and useless." 3:9

Key Elements in Titus

Teach the truth, teach sound doctrine even when it is unpopular.

Rebuke and avoid those who are false teachers.

Main Theme

Paul was making arrangements, moving people where they could do the most good, and recruiting help in the areas where he was working

Paul is the only new testament writer who quotes heathen writers.

Crete is an island in the Mediterranean Sea and is about 156 miles long and 30 miles wide. – It was known for its bad behavior.

It is believed Titus might have been from Antioch in Syria.

Paul ministered in Crete after he was released from prison in Rome. It is thought Paul may have also traveled to Spain prior to his second arrest and eventual execution. There is only limited evidence of any missionary trip by Paul to Spain.

Paul wrote to Titus from Corinth

Book 57 Philemon

Author: Paul

Date: 61 A.D.

0% Prophecy

From slave to fellow servant

Read Time: 3 Minutes

Philemon is one of four letters Paul wrote while he was in prison in Rome. These are known as the 'prison Epistles' and included Ephesians, Philippians, Colossians, and Philemon.

One of four books addressed to individuals rather than a church congregation.

Philemon is the shortest letter Paul wrote and is his only one chapter book.

Key Figures

Philemon

Onesimus

Key Events

Paul's expression of Thanksgiving.

Onesimus

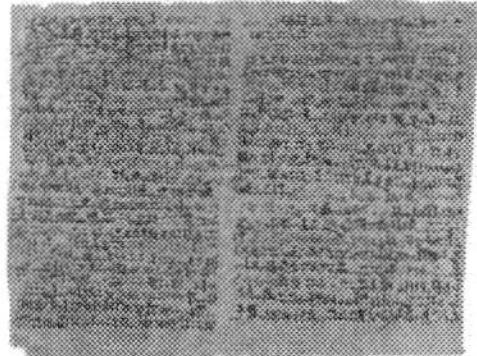

Key Verses

"Confident of your obedience, I write to you, knowing that you will do even more than I ask." 1:21

"That I appeal to you for my son Onesimus, who became my son while I was in chains." 1:10

"Yet I prefer to appeal to you on the basis of love. It is as none other than Paul – an old man and now also a prisoner of Christ Jesus" 1:9

"I am sending him – who is my very heart – back to you," 1:12

"But I did not want to do anything without your consent, so that any favor you do would not seem forced but would be voluntary." 1:14

"No longer as a slave, but better than a slave, as a dear brother. He is very dear to me but even dearer to you, both as a fellow man and as a brother in the Lord." 1:16

"So if you consider me a partner, welcome him as you would welcome me." 1:17

"If he has done you any wrong or owes you anything, charge it to me." 1:18

Key Events in Philemon

Onesimus was a slave who was owned by Philemon. At some point Onesimus fled to Rome.

While in Rome, Onesimus met Paul and was converted to Christianity.

Paul sent Onesimus back to Philemon and asked him to welcome his former slave as an equal member in the body of Christ.

Main Theme

Paul askes Philemon for a personal favor to welcome a former slave as an equal. This would have been no small request during that time period.

Under Roman law a runaway slave could be severely punished and, in some cases, even put to death.

By sending Onesimus back to Philemon he was taking the chance of sending his new friend into great danger, but Paul trusted in Philemon and that he would do the right thing.

Paul also took on any debt Onesimus might have owed in order to remove any barrier which might prevent Philemon from doing the favor for Paul.

Book 58 Hebrews

Author: Paul (Probable)

Date: 68 A.D.\

45% Prophecy

Set during the growth of the church in the Jewish community prior to 70 A.D.

Read Time: 44 Minutes

The authorship of Hebrew is not certain, but many scholars consider it the 14th Epistle of Saint Paul.

It is strongly believed the Letter to the Hebrews was intended for people living in or near Rome.

Key Figures

Jesus

Key Events

God has spoken through His son Jesus.

Jesus is superior to Angels

Jesus is the ultimate high priest

The New Covenant

Jesus' sacrifice was for all of humanity.

Key Verses

"The Son is the radiance of God's glory and the exact representation of his being, sustaining all things by his powerful word. After he had provided purification for sins, he sat down at the right hand of the Majesty in heaven." 1:3

"For the word of God is alive and active. Sharper than any double-edged sword, it penetrates even to dividing soul and spirit, joints and marrow; it judges the thoughts and attitudes of the heart." 4:12

"For we do not have a high priest who is unable to empathize with our weaknesses, but we have one who has been tempted in every way, just as we are – yet he did not sin." 4:15

"Now faith is being sure of what we hope for and certain of what we do not see." 11:1

"And without faith it is impossible to please God, because anyone who comes to him must believe that he exists and that he rewards those who earnestly seek him." 11:16

Key Elements in Hebrews

The Book of Hebrews was written to people who had been Christian for some time, but who were in danger of drifting away.

The Book of Hebrew makes strong reference to the Old Testament.

Main Theme

Jesus is the answer. He is shown to be superior to the Law of Moses which was ultimately impossible for people to maintain.

There are almost 100 references to the Old Testament in the Book of Hebrews.

It is likely the intended recipients where Jewish, or very familiar with scripture as a good understanding of Exodus and Leviticus are helpful in understanding Hebrews.

All Old Testament references are to the Septuagint version of scripture, which was the Greek translation of the original scriptures.

Book 59

James

Author: James

Date: 49 A.D.

6% Prophecy

Growth of early church among the Jews.

Read Time: 15 Minutes

James was the brother of Jesus who did not believe Jesus was the Messiah when Jesus was alive.

James became a very influential member of the church in Jerusalem following the resurrection.

The Book of James is meant for Hebrew Christians. It is addressed to the 12 tribes scattered abroad.

Key Figures

Jesus

James

Key Events

Be doers of the Word

Faith must be accompanied by actions.

Warnings about loving the things of this world.

Warnings to the rich.

Key Verses

"But be doers of the word, and not hearers only, deceiving yourselves." 1:22

"For whoever keeps the whole law and yet stumbles at just one point is guilty of breaking all of it." 2:10

"In the same way, faith by itself, if it is not accompanied by action, is dead." 2:17

"Likewise, the tongue is a small part of the body, but it makes great boasts. Consider what a great forest is set on fire by a small spark." 3:5

"But he gives us more grace. That is why Scripture says: "God opposes the proud but shows favor to the humble." 4:6

"Submit yourselves, then, to God. Resist the devil, and he will flee from you. Come near to God and he will come near to you. Wash your hands, you sinners, and purify your hearts, you double-minded." 4: 7-8

"As it is, you boast in your arrogant schemes. All such boasting is evil." 4:16

Key Elements of James

Faith must be accompanied by works or it is not true faith.

The things and the riches of this world are evil and a trap to trip up the faithful.

Main Theme

Faith without works is dead

We cannot earn our salvation by any means other than faith and the grace of God. James tells us that true faith will be shown in works. It is not the works that save a person, but works are a sign the person has been saved.

James makes up to 15 references to Jesus' Sermon on the Mount.

The Book of James is believed to be one of the first books of the New Testament to be written.

In the Book of James 'Faith' appears 12 times while 'Works' appears 13 times.

James tells us, Faith must be visible, is more than knowledge, endures trials, waits patiently, must inspire action and it must be more than just words, it must be works,

Book 60
1 Peter

Author: Peter

Date: 65 A.D.

20% Prophecy

Written during the start of persecution under Nero

Read Time: 15 Minutes

Peter was one of the original apostles called by Jesus. He was also one of the inner-circle of Apostles along with James and John.

Jesus gave Peter the keys to the kingdom of heaven. Peter opened the doors to the Jews in Acts 2, and opened the doors to the gentiles in Acts 11.

Peter was married and we know his wife sometimes travelled with him. Legend tells she and Peter were both crucified.

Key Figures

Jesus

Peter

Key Events

Keep the Faith

Do not be ashamed of faith

Expect to be persecuted

Key Verses

"In this you rejoice, though now for a little while, if necessary, you have been grieved by various trials, so that the tested genuineness of your faith—more precious than gold that perishes though it is tested by fire—may be found to result in praise and glory and honor at the revelation of Jesus Christ." 1:6-7

"Knowing that you were ransomed from the futile ways inherited from your forefathers, not with perishable things such as silver or gold, but with the precious blood of Christ, like that of a lamb without blemish or spot." 1: 18-19

"You yourselves like living stones are being built up as a spiritual house, to be a holy priesthood, to offer spiritual sacrifices acceptable to God through Jesus Christ." 2:5

"But in your hearts honor Christ the Lord as holy, always being prepared to make a defense to anyone who asks you for a reason for the hope that is in you; yet do it with gentleness and respect." 3:15

"If you are insulted for the name of Christ, you are blessed, because the Spirit of glory and of God rests upon you." 4:14

"If the righteous is scarcely saved, what will become of the ungodly and the sinner?" 4:18

Key Elements in 1 Peter

Do not be ashamed of your faith. You may be made to suffer for it, but hold fast to what you believe and your sacrifice will be pleasing to God.

Do not repay evil for evil, be patient for all things will be made right in God's time according to His plan.

Main Theme

Hold fast to your faith despite the suffering you may have to endure. You were saved by the blood of Christ and you no longer belong to this world.

1 Peter is written to Christians in a world which is becoming more and more violent toward them. While the faithful had endured hardships before, the persecution under Nero was far worse.

According to tradition Nero had Peter crucified just three years after the writing of 1 Peter. It is said Peter was crucified head down because he did not feel worthy to die in the same way as Jesus.

Peter tells us that some of us should expect to follow in the footsteps of Jesus, and Peter was to be included in this number.

Book 61
2 Peter

Author: Peter

Date: 65 A.D.

41% Prophecy

Written during the Nero Persecution.

Read Time: 10 Minutes

2 Peter was written to address false teachers within the Christian congregation who were leading the faithful to immorality.

2 Peter was written just prior to Peter's death – Tradition tells us Peter was crucified for his faith.

Key Figures

Jesus

Peter

Key Events

Great and Precious Promises

Warnings against false teachers

Exhortations to remain faithful

Key Verses

"His divine power has granted to us all things that pertain to life and godliness, through the knowledge of him who called us to his own glory and excellence, by which he has granted to us his precious and very great promises, so that through them you may become partakers of the divine nature, having escaped from the corruption that is in the world because of sinful desire." 1: 3-4

"Knowing this first of all, that no prophecy of Scripture comes from someone's own interpretation. For no prophecy was ever produced by the will of man, but men spoke from God as they were carried along by the Holy Spirit." 1:20-21

"Then the Lord knows how to rescue the godly from trials, and to keep the unrighteous under punishment until the day of judgment, and especially those who indulge in the lust of defiling passion and despise authority." 2:9

"For it would have been better for them never to have known the way of righteousness than after knowing it to turn back from the holy commandment delivered to them. What the true proverb says has happened to them: "The dog returns to its own vomit, and the sow, after washing herself, returns to wallow in the mire." 2: 21-22

Key Elements in 2 Peter

Prophets were not wrong and they were not human interpretations, we just must be patient.

There are false prophets who can and will lead the faithful away.

It is better for these people to never have known the truth than to have known the true path, then turn down a different path.

Main Theme

God's plan is perfect and all things will work out in His time and will happen according to His time line, not ours.

Peter identifies several virtues which a Christian should possess. These include Love, Godliness, Perseverance, Virtue, Knowledge, Brotherly Kindness, and Faith.

Peter was married, was an elder in the church and was one of the key leaders in the early church.

Book 62

1 John

Author: John

Date: 90 A.D.

6% Prophecy

At the time of this writing John had lived in Christ for approximately 60 years.

Read Time: 16 Minutes

John was one of the original twelve Apostles called by Jesus.

John was included in the inner circle of Apostles along with Peter and James.

John is often known as the 'disciple whom Jesus loved'.

The Apostle John authored five books of the New Testament.

Key Figures

Jesus

John

Key Events

Walk in the Light

Do not Love this world

Evidence of a true believer

The believer's victory

Key Verses

"If we confess our sins, he is faithful and just to forgive us our sins and to cleanse us from all unrighteousness. If we say we have not sinned, we make him a liar, and his word is not in us." 1: 8-9

"My little children, I am writing these things to you so that you may not sin. But if anyone does sin, we have an advocate with the Father, Jesus Christ the righteous." 2:1

"No one who abides in him keeps on sinning; no one who keeps on sinning has either seen him or known him. Little children, let no one deceive you. Whoever practices righteousness is righteous, as he is righteous." 3: 6-7

"Everyone who hates his brother is a murderer, and you know that no murderer has eternal life abiding in him." 3:15

"But if anyone has the world's goods and sees his brother in need, yet closes his heart against him, how does God's love abide in him? Little children, let us not love in word or talk but in deed and in truth." 3:17-18

"Beloved, if our heart does not condemn us, we have confidence before God; and whatever we ask we receive from him, because we keep his commandments and do what pleases him." 3: 21-22

Key Elements of 1 John

Add to the joy of believers.

Help believers guard against sin.

Confirm that the faithful have indeed overcome Satan.

Main Theme

Give strength to the faithful that their faith in Jesus and eternal life is valid and will be rewarded

The Apostle John was a vital part of the early church in Jerusalem.

It is believed John is the only one of the Apostles who did not die a violent death. It is believed John died of old age.

Written after the fall of Jerusalem in 70 A.D. and the Nero persecution, John had seen and endured a lot by the time he wrote his letters in or around 90 A.D.

While John did not suffer a martyr's death, he was not immune from suffering and persecution. He was exiled for a period of two years and he was forced to live in a cave on the Greek Island of Patmos.

Book 63

2 John

Author: John

Date: 90 A.D.

15% Prophecy

Remain steadfast in faith.

Read Time: 2 Minutes

John was one of the original twelve Apostles called by Jesus.

John was included in the inner circle of Apostles along with Peter and James.

John is often known as the 'disciple whom Jesus loved'.

The Apostle John authored five books of the New Testament.

It is believed John is the only one of the Apostles who did not die a violent death. It is believed John died of old age

Key Figures

Jesus

John

Key Elements

Love One Another

Key Verses

"I rejoiced greatly to find some of your children walking in the truth, just as we were commanded by the Father." 1:4

"And now I ask you, dear lady—not as though I were writing you a new commandment, but the one we have had from the beginning—that we love one another." 1:5

"And this is love, that we walk according to his commandments; this is the commandment, just as you have heard from the beginning, so that you should walk in it." 1:6

"For many deceivers have gone out into the world, those who do not confess the coming of Jesus Christ in the flesh. Such a one is the deceiver and the antichrist. Watch yourselves, so that you may not lose what we have worked for, but may win a full reward." 1: 7-8

"Everyone who goes on ahead and does not abide in the teaching of Christ, does not have God. Whoever abides in the teaching has both the Father and the Son." 1:9

"If anyone comes to you and does not bring this teaching, do not receive him into your house or give him any greeting, for whoever greets him takes part in his wicked works." 1: 10-11

Key Elements in 2 John

Take pride in others faith

Do not be deceived

Remain true to your faith

Main Theme

Love one another as God has and continues to love you.

The Book of 2 John is one of the shortest books of the Bible and can be read in just 2 minutes. However, it contains the very basic truths of faith. Love one another, remain true to what you have been taught and stay the course.

John was one of the three Apostles who were allowed to see Jesus when He was transfigured. Along with Peter and James they had the unique opportunity to see Jesus as we will someday see Him.

2 John is just one of five Books in the Bible to be only one chapter in length.

2 John stressed truth, love, and obedience. It warned against the antichrist, false teachers and not following God's commandments.

2 John was probably written while John was living in Ephesus.

Book 64
3 John

Author: John

Date: 90 A.D.

0% Prophecy

Concerns Christian Hospitality

Read Time: 2 Minutes

John was one of the original twelve Apostles called by Jesus.

John was included in the inner circle of Apostles along with Peter and James.

John is often known as the 'disciple whom Jesus loved'.

The Apostle John authored five books of the New Testament.

It is believed John is the only one of the Apostles who did not die a violent death. It is believed John died of old age

Key Figures

John

Key Elements

Helping Others

Benediction

Key Verses

"It gave me great joy when some believers came and testified about your faithfulness to the truth, telling how you continue to walk in it." 1:3

I wrote to the church, but Diotrephes, who loves to be first, will not welcome us. So when I come, I will call attention to what he is doing, spreading malicious nonsense about us. Not satisfied with that, he even refuses to welcome other believers. He also stops those who want to do so and puts them out of the church." 1: 9-10

"Do not imitate what is evil but what is good. Anyone who does what is good is from God. Anyone who does what is evil has not seen God. Demetrius is well spoken of by everyone—and even by the truth itself. We also speak well of him, and you know that our testimony is true." 1: 11-12

"I have much to write you, but I do not want to do so with pen and ink. I hope to see you soon, and we will talk face to face." 1: 13-14

Key Elements of 3 John

Christians should be ready to help one another.

Beware false teachers

Main Theme

Have nothing to do with false teachers

3 John is the shortest Book in the Bible.

In 3 John the Apostle John makes no mention of Jesus.

Diotrephes was attempting to dominate the early church and one reason for the writing of 3 John was to reassure people that John would deal with the problem when he arrived.

John is seen as the Apostle who proclaimed love one another, but in 3 John we see he can be a strong leader as he promises to deal with the problem and calling out the wrong doer.

3 John was written in Ephesus and was delivered by Demetrius.

Book 65 Jude

Author: Jude

Date: 68-75 A.D.

40% Prophecy

Written around the time of the destruction of Jerusalem

Read Time: 4 Minutes

Jude was one of Jesus' brothers, was called Judas in Matthew and Mark.

Jude and James were the only two of Jesus's brothers who wrote books which are included in the Bible.

Jude is not directed to a particular group of people or geographic region.

Key Figures

Jesus

Jude

Key Elements

Warnings from the History of the Ungodly

Second coming of Jesus

Keep yourselves within the love of God

Key Verses

"For certain individuals whose condemnation was written about long ago have secretly slipped in among you. They are ungodly people, who pervert the grace of our God into a license for immorality and deny Jesus Christ our only Sovereign and Lord." 1:4

"Though you already know all this, I want to remind you that the Lord at one time delivered his people out of Egypt, but later destroyed those who did not believe." 1:5

"And the angels who did not keep their positions of authority but abandoned their proper dwelling – these he has kept in darkness, bound with everlasting chains for judgment on the great Day." 1:6

"In a similar way, Sodom and Gomorrah and the surrounding towns gave themselves up to sexual immorality and perversion. They serve as an example of those who suffer the punishment of eternal fire." 1:7

"In the last time there will be scoffers, following their own ungodly passions. It is these who cause divisions, worldly people, devoid of the Spirit." 1: 18-19

Key Elements in Jude

Jude condemns the people who are leading the faithful astray. He uses some very vivid history to remind them God does not look away from evil forever.

Main Theme

Stand firm in your faith and what you know to be true. Even though times are hard, God always keeps His promises.

Jude is the only record of an angle disputing Satan concerning the body of Moses. "*But even the archangel Michael, when he was disputing with the devil about the body of Moses, did not himself dare to condemn him for slander but said, "The Lord rebuke you!" 1:9*

[Moses was buried in an unmarked grave just before the people of Israel entered the Promised Land.]

Jude's benediction is considered one of the most beautiful in the Bible.

Book 66 Revelation

Author: John

Date: 95 A.D.

95% Prophecy

Written to tell us about the end of days and the second coming of Jesus

Read Time: 1 Hour 1 Min.

Revelation comes from a Greek word meaning to unveil.

John was exiled to the island of Patmos which is in the Aegean Sea, 24 miles west of Asia Minor.

The Apostle John is estimated to be 90 years old at the time he wrote the Book of Revelation.

Key Figures

Jesus

John

Satan

Key Events

Seven Letters to the seven churches of Asia

Seven seals, seven trumpets, and seven bowls of wrath.

Key Verses

"The revelation of Jesus Christ, which God gave him to show to his servants the things that must soon take place. He made it known by sending his angel to his servant John." 1:1

"who bore witness to the word of God and to the testimony of Jesus Christ, even to all that he saw" 1:2

"Behold, he is coming with the clouds, and every eye will see him, even those who pierced him, and all tribes of the earth will wail on account of him. Even so. Amen." 1:7

"And they have conquered him by the blood of the Lamb and by the word of their testimony, for they loved not their lives even unto death." 12:11

"And I heard a loud voice from the throne saying, "Behold, the dwelling place of God is with man. He will dwell with them, and they will be his people, and God himself will be with them as their God." 21:3

"He will wipe away every tear from their eyes, and death shall be no more, neither shall there be mourning, nor crying, nor pain anymore, for the former things have passed away." 21:4

"will see his face, and his name will be on [our] *foreheads" 22:4*

Key Elements in the Book of Revelation

The opening sentence makes it clear what the letter will be concerning.

There are seven letters to the seven churches of Asia contained within the Book of Revelation.

Main Theme

God and Jesus win in the end, Satan and the demons of this world cannot and will not win the ultimate final battle.

Rome had for decades ignored Christianity because they considered it a part of the Jewish faith. When Christianity was deemed its own religion, it was made illegal.

Revelation was written during a time of great oppression and cruelty to Christians.

Out of 404 verses in Revelation, 278 of them make a reference to the Old Testament.

The seven churches of Asia are; Ephesus, Smyma, Pergamum, Thyatira, Sardis, Philadelphia and Laodicea.

Revelation is believed to be the last book of the Bible to be written.

APOCRYPHA BOOKS

These are also known as Deuterocanonical books.

Baruch

Author: Baruch (?)

Date: 6th Century B.C.

Baruch is one of seven books included in what is called the Apocrypha Books. This group of seven books was included in most biblical text for approximately 1,500 years. When the Protestant church broke away from the Catholic Church these seven books were removed from the Protestant Bible. The books remain in the Catholic Bible. These books include Baruch, Wisdom of Solomon, Sirach, 1 Maccabees, 2 Maccabees, Tobit and Judith.

Baruch lived in the 6th century B.C. and was the scribe or secretary for the prophet Jeremiah.

Most scholars agree Baruch came from a prominent family and since he acted as a scribe he was obviously well educated.

Baruch was with Jeremiah during the very turbulent years just before the fall of Jerusalem in 587 B.C.

There is a great deal of debate if Baruch is the actual author of this book.

Key Verses

"And you shall say: The Lord our God is in the right, but there is open shame on us today, on the people of Judah, on the inhabitants of Jerusalem, and on our kings, our rulers, our priests, our prophets, and our ancestors, because we have sinned before the Lord. We have disobeyed him, and have not heeded the voice of the Lord our God, to walk in the statutes of the Lord that he set before us" 1:15-18

"Yet you have dealt with us, O Lord our God, in all your kindness and in all your great compassion" 2:27

"Take courage, my children, and cry to God, for you will be remembered by the one who brought this upon you. For just as you were disposed to go astray from God, return with tenfold zeal to seek him. For the one who brought these calamities upon you will bring you everlasting joy with your salvation." 4:27-29

"Take off the garment of affliction, O Jerusalem, and put on forever the beauty of the glory from God. Put on the robe of righteousness that comes from God" 5:1

Key Elements of Baruch

Baruch encouraged the people to be pro-Babylonian. Not only did he consider resistance futile, but he felt it was God's desire that the people be in exile.

Main Theme

Even though they are suffering and have been taken prisoner, the people must believe God will not forget them and will come to their rescue.

According to the Septuagint, Baruch took over the duties of Jeremiah after his death and thus became a sage rather than a scribe. What eventually became of Baruch is unknown.

Archaeologist have found many bulla's in Israel. A Bulla is a dollop of clay in which a seal was pressed to mark an official document. They found a large number of bulla bearing the seals of royal officials of Judah. Among these was a bulla with the name of Baruch. This would seem to offer proof of Baruch acting as a scribe, perhaps for Jeremiah.

Wisdom Or Wisdom of Solomon

Author: Unknown

Date: 200 B.C.

Wisdom is one of seven books included in what is called the Apocrypha Books. This group of seven books was included in most biblical text for approximately 1,500 years. When the Protestant church broke away from the Catholic Church these seven books were removed from the Protestant Bible. The books remain in the Catholic Bible. These books include Baruch, Wisdom of Solomon, Sirach, 1 Maccabees, 2 Maccabees, Tobit and Judith.

Given its title it would be easy to assume the author of this book was Solomon. However, since there are many references made to the Septuagint which was not written until 300 B.C. it is obvious Solomon is not the author. – It should be noted the author never claims to be Solomon, but does not give their name.

Key Verses

"The ungodly ... reasoned unsoundly, saying to themselves,...
we were born by mere chance, and hereafter we shall be as though we had never been, for the breath in our nostrils is smoke, and reason is a spark kindled by the beating of our hearts
when it is extinguished, the body will turn to ashes, and the spirit will dissolve like empty air.:" 2:1-3

"Thus they reasoned, but they were led astray, ...
for God created us for incorruption, and made us in the image of his own eternity." 2: 21-23

"What has our arrogance profited us? And what good has our boasted wealth brought us? All those things have vanished like a shadow, and like a rumor that passes by." 5:8

"Wisdom is radiant and unfading, and she is easily discerned by those who love her" 6:12

"For wickedness, of its nature cowardly, testifies in its own condemnation, and because of a distressed conscience, always magnifies misfortunes." 17:11

Key Elements of Wisdom

Fools believe there is no God, no soul, and no eternity.

We have been made in God's image and wisdom shows us we will have eternal life with God if we remain faithful.

Riches of this world are useless.

Main Theme

The author is attempting to show the vast difference between the way the world thinks, and the way God is. The world is full of foolishness, while God is Wisdom.

In the Book of Wisdom, the author attempts to show that wisdom is an intermediary between God and man. Since God is so superior to man that we cannot possibly understand His ways or His ultimate plan, we have been given wisdom to help us understand what we need to do and how we need to live. The Book of Wisdom makes it very clear idolatry is evil and the way of the foolish. Wisdom is found through prayer and was important in the understanding of the person of Jesus.

Sirach

Author: Ben Sira

Date: 200-180 B.C.

The Book of Sirach is known by many names. These include Sira, Wisdom of Jesus the son of Sirach, and also as Ecclesiasticus which could mean 'church book'.

Sirach is one of seven books included in what is called the Apocrypha Books. This group of seven books was included in most biblical text for approximately 1,500 years. When the Protestant church broke away from the Catholic Church these seven books were removed from the Protestant Bible. The books remain in the Catholic Bible. These books include Baruch, Wisdom of Solomon, Sirach, 1 Maccabees, 2 Maccabees, Tobit and Judith.

The Book of Sirach was originally written in Hebrew and translated to Greek in 117 B.C.

Sirach is the longest of the Apocrypha Books

Ben Sira was a scribe and religious teacher in Jerusalem.

Key Verses

"Another goes his way a weakling and a failure, with little strength and great misery—Yet the eyes of the Lord look favorably upon him; he raises him free of the vile dust." 11:12

"Prepare your words and you will be listened to; draw upon your training, and then give your answer" 33:4

"The pride of the height is the firmament in its clearness, The appearance of heaven, in the spectacle of its glory." 43:1

"At the word of the Holy One they will stand in due order, And they will not faint in their watches." 43:10

"When you glorify the Lord, exalt him as much as you can; For even yet he will exceed: And when you exalt him, put forth your full strength: Be not weary; for you will never attain." 43:30

"During his lifetime, [Elisha] feared no one, nor was any man able to intimidate his will" 48:12

Key Elements in Sirach

Wealth attained apart from God's will is meaningless.

Seek wisdom and praise God

Main Theme

Ben Sira does not want his students/followers to just be successful in the eyes of the world, but more importantly in the eyes of God.

Ben Sira was a very devote Jew and believed in the Jewish way of life. He wanted to preserve the Torah and the ministry of the Temple in Jerusalem.

Ben Sira speaks a great deal about women in this book, but most references are in a negative tone. A daughter is seen as a loss to the father as she will likely commit sexual improprieties.

The Book of Sirach is broken up into blocks of short stories or sayings which encourage the reader to constantly seek the wisdom of the Lord.

The Book of Sirach should not be confused with the Book of Ecclesiastes which is considered canonical by almost all Christians.

1 Maccabees

Author: Uncertain

Date: 1st Century B.C.

---

1 Maccabees is one of seven books included in what is called the Apocrypha Books. This group of seven books was included in most biblical text for approximately 1,500 years. When the Protestant church broke away from the Catholic Church these seven books were removed from the Protestant Bible. The books remain in the Catholic Bible. These books include Baruch, Wisdom of Solomon, Sirach, 1 Maccabees, 2 Maccabees, Tobit and Judith.

The Maccabees were a group of Jewish fighters who assumed power in Israel in the second century B.C. The group led a rebellion against Antiochus IV and consecrated the Temple of Jerusalem.

When they consecrated the Temple,

the Temple menorah burned for eight days instead of one. This miracle is celebrated on the holiday of Chanukah.

Key Verses

"In those days went there out of Israel wicked men, who persuaded many, saying, Let us go and make a covenant with the heathen that are round about us: for since we departed from them we have had much sorrow." 1:11

"Even if all the nations that live under the rule of the king obey him, and have chosen to obey his commandments, every one of them abandoning the religion of their ancestors, I and my sons and my brothers will continue to live by the covenant of our ancestors. Far be it from us to desert the law and the ordinances. We will not obey the king's words by turning aside from our religion." 2: 19-22

"Do not fear the words of sinners, for their splendor will turn into dung and worms. Today they will be exalted, but tomorrow they will not be found, because they will have returned to the dust, and their plans will have perished."2:62-63

Key Elements of 1 Maccabees

People were allowing the Syrian rulers to influence their lives and lead them away from God.

The revolt was to maintain a Jewish way of life and to take back the country and the Temple.

Main Theme

1 Maccabees deals with the historical elements of the revolt.

2 Maccabees deals with the religious nature of the revolt.

According to the historian Josephus the rebels originally refused to fight on the Sabot and as a result in the first battle 1,000 of their people were slaughtered, including a great many women and children.

The Maccabees then proclaimed the Jewish faith was a faith of the living and declared it was right and just to do battle on the sabot to preserve the life of believers.

2 Maccabees

Author: Uncertain

Date: 1st Century B.C.

---

2 Maccabees is one of seven books included in what is called the Apocrypha Books. This group of seven books was included in most biblical text for approximately 1,500 years. When the Protestant church broke away from the Catholic Church these seven books were removed from the Protestant Bible. The books remain in the Catholic Bible. These books include Baruch, Wisdom of Solomon, Sirach, 1 Maccabees, 2 Maccabees, Tobit and Judith.

The Maccabees were a group of Jewish fighters who assumed power in Israel in the second century B.C. The group led a rebellion against Antiochus IV and consecrated the Temple of Jerusalem.

When they consecrated the Temple the Temple menorah burned for eight days instead of one. This miracle is celebrated on the holiday of Chanukah.

Key Verses

"Since we have been saved by God from grave dangers, we give him great thanks as befits those who fought against the king." 1:11

"Gather together our scattered people, free those who are slaves among the Gentiles, look kindly on those who are despised and detested, and let the Gentiles know that you are our God." 1:27

Then the Lord will disclose these things, and the glory of the Lord and the cloud will be seen, just as they appeared in the time of Moses and of Solomon when he prayed that the place might be greatly sanctified." 2:8*

"God never withdraws his mercy from us. Although he disciplines us with misfortunes, he does not abandon his own people. Let these words suffice for recalling this truth." 6:6

"But doubtless the Creator of the world, who formed the generation of man, and found out the beginning of all things, will also of his own mercy give you breath and life again, as ye now regard not your own selves for his laws' sake." 7:23

Key Elements of 2 Maccabees

People were allowing the Syrian rulers to influence their lives and lead them away from God.

The revolt was to maintain a Jewish way of life and to take back the country and the Temple.

Main Theme

1 Maccabees deals with the historical elements of the revolt.

2 Maccabees deals with the religious nature of the revolt.

It is interesting that the Book of 2 Maccabees tells us what happened to the Ark of the Covenant. It was taken out of the city and hidden by Jeremiah. It was said it would not be found until such time as God allowed and desired it to be found.

"It was also contained in the same writing, that the prophet, being warned of God, commanded the tabernacle and the ark to go with him, as he went forth into the mountain, where Moses climbed up, and saw the heritage of God." 2:4

Tobit

Author: Unknown

Date: 300-200 B.C.

Tobit is one of seven books included in what is called the Apocrypha Books. This group of seven books was included in most biblical text for approximately 1,500 years. When the Protestant church broke away from the Catholic Church these seven books were removed from the Protestant Bible. The books remain in the Catholic Bible. These books include Baruch, Wisdom of Solomon, Sirach, 1 Maccabees, 2 Maccabees, Tobit and Judith.

The Book of Tobit takes on the feel of one of Jesus' parables. The messenger is a real person and the moral of the story is true and important.

The story revolves around the character of Tobit and Sarah who are forced to endure many hardships including blindness.

In ancient times blindness was seen as the result of sin and the removal of God's blessing. It could be the sin of the person, or an ancestor who sinned.

Key Verses

"At that time the prayers of them both were heard in the sight of the glory of the most high God:
And the holy angel of the Lord, Raphael was sent to heal them both, whose prayers at one time were rehearsed in the sight of the Lord." 3: 24-25

"Then the angel Raphael took the devil, and bound him in the desert of upper Egypt." 8:3

"Good is prayer with fasting, alms, and righteousness. A little with righteousness is better than much with unrighteousness. It is better to give alms than to lay up gold." 12:8

"For I am the angel Raphael, one of the seven who stand before the Lord." 12:15

"Give thanks to the Lord with goodness, and bless the everlasting King, that his tabernacle may be built in you again with joy, and that he may make glad in you those who are captives, and love in you forever those who are miserable." 13:10

"And after he had lived ninety-nine years in the fear of the Lord, with joy they buried him." 14:16

Key Elements of Tobit

Tobit and Sara undergo many hardships.

Both remain loyal to the Lord.

Tobit and Sara are healed and live a long good life.

Main Theme

God is just and fair in all of His dealings

To some there is a similarity between the story of Tobit and Job. Suffering character who remains true to God and is eventually cured and rewarded.

Five fragments of Tobit were found in the Dead Sea Scrolls.

Athanasius (Bishop of Alexandria in the 4th Century) said that certain books, including the book of Tobit, while not part of the Canon, "were appointed by the Fathers" to be read.

Tobit is a love story which shows that prayer and steadfastness will prevail over evil, and God will send help when it is needed. Although not always an angel.

Judith

Author: Palestinian Jew

Date: 100 B.C.

Judith is one of seven books included in what is called the Apocrypha Books. This group of seven books was included in most biblical text for approximately 1,500 years. When the Protestant church broke away from the Catholic Church these seven books were removed from the Protestant Bible. The books remain in the Catholic Bible. These books include Baruch, Wisdom of Solomon, Sirach, 1 Maccabees, 2 Maccabees, Tobit and Judith.

The Book of Judith takes place in Assyria before Nebuchadnezzar became king.

Some scholars point out there are potential historical inaccuracies in the Book of Judith. It is unclear if these are legitimate errors, or errors in transmission or our understanding of history from 2,100 years ago.

One reason Judith may not be in the canon is because she did not behave like a typical 1st Century woman.

Key Verses

"And every man of Israel cried to God with great earnestness, and with great earnestness they humbled their souls." 4:9

"No one had a bad word to say about her, for she was a very God-fearing woman." 8:8

"Besides all this let's give thanks to the Lord our God, who tries us, even as he did our fathers also." 8:25

"Then Judith said to them, "Hear me, and I will do a thing, which will go down to all generations among the children of our race." 8:32

"Your strength is not in numbers, nor does your power depend upon stalwart men; but you are the God of the lowly, the helper of the oppressed, the supporter of the weak, the protector of the forsaken, the savior of those without hope." 9:11

"A single Hebrew woman has brought disgrace on the house of King Nebuchadnezzar. Here is Holofernes headless on the ground!" 14:18

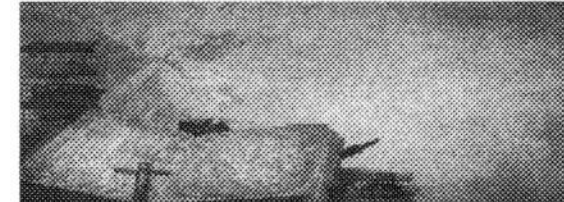

Key Elements of Judith

Military Maneuvering of Nebuchadnezzar

Judith saves Israel

Main Theme

The nation of Israel is in danger from the Babylonians and is saved by the actions of Judith.

Judith used her beauty and feminine charm to seduce and then decapitate the opposing general Holofernes to save her city.

Critics say Judith was wrong for dressing as a man, then tricking her enemy before killing them. Others see her as a brave and cunning warrior who did what was needed to survive and protect her people.

Some believe Judith was too sexy and far too radical to be included in the Canon. Her behavior was inappropriate for a woman of her time.

No copies or remnants of the Book of Judith were found in the Dead Sea Scrolls.

Additional Apocrypha Books which are either widely rejected or have been accepted on a limited basis.

In addition to the books of Baruch, Wisdom of Solomon, Sirach, 1 Maccabees, 2 Maccabees, Tobit and Judith there are additional Apocrypha Books.

The most accepted of these books is the Book known as **Bel and the Dragon**. In some traditional biblical texts, the Book of Bel and the Dragon is included as chapter 14 in the book of Daniel. In the Protestant Bible the Book of Daniel ends with chapter 12.

The book is centered upon the existence of a dragon-god in Babylon. There is no other mention of this idol but some believe it is relevant because of dragon prophecies of the last days.

Other books are not nearly as accepted and are in fact widely rejected. Looking at the best known five of these, two of them are associated with the Book of Daniel.

The Song of the Three Holy Children is an addition to the Book of Daniel written sometime around 100 B.C. It was found inserted in the Book of Daniel in the third chapter.

The History of Susanna is a prefix to the Book of Daniel and seems intended to highlight Daniel's powers and judgement.

1 Esdras is at least in part the Greek version of the Book of Ezra and was written around 100 B.C. Some material in the book comes from the Book of Nehemiah.

2 Esdras focuses on the period around the fall of Jerusalem in 70 A.D. It is believed to have been written prior to 120 A.D.

The Prayer of Manasses was written around 100 B.C. and revolves around the Babylonian captivity. Portions of this prayer can be found in Protestant liturgy.

Apocrypha - biblical related writings which are not part of the accepted canon.

Deuterocanonical - sacred books or literary works which can or may form a secondary canon.

The percentage of prophecy of the books is calculated by taking the number of verses in the book which mention any type of prophecy or coming event and dividing it by the total number of verses in the individual book.

Reading time is estimated based on the reading speed of the average individual. Reading time will vary depending on how fast or slow you read and different translations will have different word counts.

Made in United States
Orlando, FL
06 May 2024

46580486R00098